INVESTING
IN THE FUTURE

10 New Industries and over 75 Key Growth
Companies That Are Changing the Face
of Corporate America

INVESTING
IN THE FUTURE

10 New Industries and over 75 Key Growth
Companies That Are Changing the Face
of Corporate America

KIRIL SOKOLOFF
JOSEPH E. LAIRD
THOMAS H. MACK

Doubleday & Company, Inc., Garden City, New York
1982

The authors specifically disclaim any personal liability, loss, or risk incurred as a consequence of the use and application, either directly or indirectly, of any advice or information contained herein.

Library of Congress Cataloging in Publication Data

Sokoloff, Kiril.
Investing in the future.

Includes index.
1. Investments — United States.   2. United States —
Industries.   3. Corporations — United States.   I. Laird,
Joseph E.   II. Mack, Thomas H.   III. Title.
HG4921.S616   332.6′712
AACR2
ISBN 0-385-17759-3
Library of Congress Catalog Card Number: 81 – 43858

ACKNOWLEDGMENTS

The authors would particularly like to thank their many friends and associates who gave unstintingly of their time and knowledge in the preparation of this book. In that regard, the authors would like to make special mention of the help provided by Bruce E. Lazier, Eli S. Lustgarten, Stuart M. Robbins, Thomas A. Escott, Marion B. Stewart, David MacCallum, Frederick Prunier, Lee S. Isgur, John B. Walker, Robert T. Cornell, Sanford J. Garrett, Bradford L. Peery, John V. Pincavage, Margo N. Alexander, Barbara S. Isgur, Gil Schwartz, J. Kendrick Noble, and Edward A. Jones. We are particularly indebted to Frederick Meserve for his thinking on demographic trends. Thanks also to Charles L. Grimes and Robert Gutenstein for reading the manuscript and making many valuable suggestions.

Contents

Contents

List of Exhibits

An Early Word About Timing

In this book we plan to cover the industries that look promising for the 1980s and the companies that are well positioned in those industries. We do not discuss the stocks of those companies and that is an intentional omission.

There is a world of difference between stocks and companies. As so often happens, the underlying business of a company may be way out of line with its current stock price. Perhaps investors are too optimistic about a company's prospects and bid the stock price beyond a reasonable level of value. Or perhaps an industry goes from the height of fashion to investor disfavor in a matter of months. Such events can have a dramatic effect on the price of a stock — even if the underlying fundamentals of the company have not changed at all.

Two examples will illustrate what we mean. During 1980 the stock of Tandy Corp., one of the companies we discuss in the book, was one of the best performers on the New York Stock Exchange, tripling in value. But over the course of that year Tandy's stock was often subject to sharp, short-term price declines. One associate of ours characterized Tandy as a stock not for the faint of heart. The oil service and domestic oil and gas companies, which are also covered in the book, were stellar performers between 1978 and 1980. During the 1978 – 80 period, many stocks in this group rose three to fivefold, or more. But then in 1981, as fears of an oil glut mounted and disinflation worries grew, these stocks lost anywhere from 40 to 60 percent of their value.

Such volatility is particularly difficult to deal with for authors of a book on business and investments. Between the time a book is written and published, many months elapse, and stock valuations can alter dramatically in the meantime. Furthermore, by their very nature, books have a longer term perspective than most other sources of business information. In fact, a business book may often be read several years after it was written. In the interim, stock valuations may have changed so dramatically that what was once grossly undervalued has now become grossly overvalued, and vice versa.

For all these reasons, we have felt that, in the final analysis, the book would be most useful to the reader if we limited the discussion to the long-term outlook for certain industries and companies. The valuation of the stock at the time of proposed purchase, and whether the stock is a good investment at that price, is a subject that we will leave for readers to decide for themselves.

It may be useful to make an up-front comment about the economic and overall stock market environment. It is becoming increasingly likely that the country is entering a period of disinflation, which, at first, will prove to be a mixed blessing. The pain associated with reducing inflation may prove excruciating, and the transition process may take some years. Ultimately, reduced inflationary expectations will allow our economy to have a period of sustained real economic growth. Equally important, disinflation will encourage a switch from investing in tangible assets like real estate and gold to common stocks and bonds. When you read this book, the economy and the stock market may well be in the final throes of the transition to disinflation. Even though stocks may be down sharply and the economy look as if it may not recover, don't lose sight of the long-term benefits of a lower rate of inflation.

The disinflation journey will be difficult for almost every company in America. It is impossible to gauge, at this writing, all the effects of disinflation on the companies mentioned in this book. Suffice it to say that the weakened financial condition of all companies makes careful company and stock analysis a prerequisite. In the next few years, preservation of capital and productive employment of capital may become the prime considerations of investors. For too long, there has been a flagrant disregard for capital, and a return to investment conservatism will be a healthy step.

So long as the transition to disinflation does not create a financial crisis that runs out of control, the stock market should bottom by autumn of 1982 or early 1983. While investor gloom may be over-powering when you read this book, remember that major bottoms are made in periods of crisis and despair. Forty years of inflation, the accumulation of over five trillion dollars of debt, and unprecedentedly leveraged corporate and consumer balance sheets cannot be easily or painlessly unwound. The nation has been geared up for more inflation and is discovering to its horror that disinflation, even some deflation, is on the way.

Some experts think that inflation cannot be ended by the Federal Reserve alone. But there is precedent for it. After the inflation of World War I, the Fed clamped down on credit and in a year and a half was able to root out inflation so dramatically that the nation did not have any inflation for twenty-five years. It is possible that we, too, may be near to long-lasting relief from inflation. For those who are not heavily in debt and have lots of cash reserves in the form of Treasury bills, the opportunities created by the transition to disinflation should be considerable.

It is for this reason that we have concentrated on companies that should be able to generate unit volume growth. In a disinflationary environment full of competitive pricing, the best chance at increasing profits may well come from selling more units.

Kiril Sokoloff
Joseph E. Laird
Thomas H. Mack

CHAPTER 1

How This Book Can Help You

In Cincinnati, Ohio, the Talbot family can see the wave of the future on their TV set. An advanced cable TV system brings the Talbots forty-six different channels offering everything from news to culture to "Nickelodeon," a program of cartoon characters who teach young children to read. The Talbots also have a two-way, interactive connection that allows them to register their views about current events, television shows, or a presidential speech.

In homes all over the country, people of every age flick a switch on electronic devices and transform their TV screens into exciting video games. Spaceships fight against flying saucers or attempt to get through complex defense systems to eliminate an enemy base. Among their other options are football games, baseball games, tank warfare, mazes, monsters, and much more.

In Tampa, Florida, the Fernandez family sits down to eat dinner in front of the TV. But instead of the nightly fare of network programming, they watch a late movie recorded a week ago on their videocassette recorder. The next night they'll rent a videotape of *Star Wars* for less than one quarter of what it would cost to take the family to the movies.

Helen Thompson, an executive secretary at a large corporation in New York City, now does her typing in front of a TV-like screen. Everything she types is electronically stored, and paragraphs, words, or punctuation can be changed without her having to retype an entire page.

In a Chrysler K-car plant in Delaware, an automated body-welding system now does the work of human welders. The result: production of cars has increased from fifty an hour to sixty-five and at less cost.

In an increasing number of locations across the country, people are receiving hospital care from efficient, well-managed hospital chains rather than from traditional voluntary or community hospitals.

The energy capitals of the country, like Houston, Dallas, and Denver, are experiencing a strong economy despite recession, while old industrial towns, such as Detroit and Cleveland, are losing jobs, population, and industry.

In New York City, John Appleby, a lawyer in a top law firm, is faced with a predicament: he must get a draft of a contract to his client within twenty-four hours. A quick visit to the nearest office of Federal Express and the envelope is on its way to a guaranteed overnight delivery.

The busy Washington lobbyist always used to take the Eastern Airlines shuttle when he needed to visit his corporate clients in New York. Now, he flies on a new commuter airline.

The Pasadena *Star News,* a subsidiary of Knight-Ridder Newspapers in California, is spending over $2 million to purchase the latest in press technology from Information International, Inc. In effect, the new system will permit a fully computerized assembly and layout of all the stories, pictures, and advertisements that make up the newspaper. This is called electronic pagination, and if it were adopted by the nation's 1,745 daily newspapers, it could save the industry more than $2 billion a year.

There are 110 million residential and 50 million business telephones in this country and one third of those phones turn over every year. Up until now, the replacement market was filled by essentially the same type of phone that has been used for nearly a century. Some might think the revolution in technology had passed the telephone by completely; if you're one of them, take another look. The electronic telephone is here.

The business executive, the small business owner, the investor, the professional, the lawyer, the doctor, and the accountant (to name only a few) are all victims of information overload. The problem today is not how much information is available, but rather how to obtain the particular information you need for your business, investments, or profession. Electronics is coming to the rescue with customized information services. For example, Knight-Ridder's commodity news wire breaks down its information flow into twenty categories.

Instead of going shopping for a new set of china at a local department store, Carol Jones tunes her TV set to the "Shopping Channel," the latest cable TV experiment in video shopping. When the attractive host shows her a piece of china that she likes, Carol dials a toll-free 800 number to place her order, at a 30 percent discount.

Bob Franklin has noticed a strange phenomenon in retailing. Whenever he visits the local Sears or Kmart, he finds the stores surprisingly empty. But when he takes his son to a nearby toy store, he finds a mob of people.

At first glance, these vignettes appear totally unrelated, but in reality they are linked in one important way. All of them illustrate major new trends in American business. We are on the threshold of good growth opportunities in ten new industries, and certain companies in these industries are likely to achieve large increases in unit sales, the best long-term determinant of business and investment success.

The impact of these changes, as the examples above suggest, goes far beyond business and investment opportunities. Some of the most basic aspects of American life are undergoing a radical transformation. What's happening now is as important as the mass production of the automobile was in the early part of this century and the introduction of the TV set to the home was in the 1950s.

The ten industries we'll examine are being fueled by events in four areas. First, technology (specifically electronics) is invading the home, the office, and the factory. Second, deregulation by the government in recent years has changed the rules of the game to a greater extent than at any time in the last four decades. Not only are industries representing nearly half of the U.S. gross national product (GNP) being deregulated, but the tax law now makes savings and investment relatively more attractive as well. Third, petroleum, the world's most widely used commodity, experienced a major shortage and a thirteenfold price increase in a decade, two developments which have improved the economics of energy exploration in this

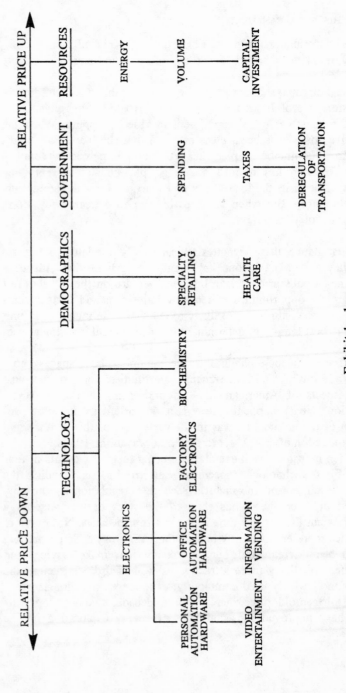

Exhibit 1 – 1
Beneficiaries of relative price changes.

country. Fourth, the distribution of goods and consumer spending patterns are changing radically because certain industrial groups and certain parts of the country are growing faster than others.

Exhibit 1–1 shows how these factors interconnect with our ten new industries. Technology is creating five of the ten industries: personal automation hardware, video entertainment, office automation hardware, information vending, and factory electronics. The government, through deregulation of the transportation industry, is benefiting certain aggressive transportation companies. The high price of energy has spurred two industries: energy exploration and energy services. Finally, changing distribution / consumption patterns are causing a boom in specialty retailing and professionally managed chains of health care delivery. These ten industries are discussed below.

PERSONAL AUTOMATION HARDWARE

By 1990 the television set, which in 1981 was watched approximately seven hours a day by the average American family, will change from a passive device to an active one. Through the proliferation of videocassette recorders, videodisc recorders, and cable TV hookups, we will be able to watch what we want, where we want, when we want.

The home computer will also come into its own in this decade. Because of the growing number and complexity of electronic items in the home — cable TV; sophisticated telephones, home security, energy cost control, and video games — the demand for a central, computer-based system is bound to increase.

The volume opportunities in personal automation hardware are considerable. By the end of the decade, we estimate that over 100 million videocassette and videodisc recorders will have been sold and perhaps as many as 10 million home computers.

VIDEO ENTERTAINMENT

While the hardware business is going to boom, even greater opportunities lie in software — that is, in the entertainment, information, educational material, financial transactions, and shopping facilities that will flow through these millions of hardware units. We estimate the software side of the business may eventually be as much as ten times as large as the hardware market. That's because software is consumed and therefore must be replaced. Once you purchase a videocassette recorder, that's it (at least, for a while). But the money that is spent on rented tape cassettes and special movies on cable TV will keep on rising, as the software selection increases and more people purchase the hardware.

If the future demand for software is as strong as we think, it might account for at least 4 percent of personal spending in the United States by the end of the decade. More importantly, the portion of that spending devoted to video-related communications might rise from around 5 percent in 1980 to between 20 and 40 percent by the end of the decade. Therefore, by 1990 the market for software might be $35 – 75 billion a year.

OFFICE AUTOMATION HARDWARE

Some analysts estimate that each farm worker in this country is backed by $52,000 of capital investment and each industrial worker by $37,000 — but each office worker by only $2,500. That should give something of an idea of the volume opportunities for this industry.

If the over 18 million office workers were backed by, say, $10,000 of capital, we'd have a market of $180 billion. And capital investment equaling that of industrial workers would generate sales volume in excess of $500 billion. No matter what the ultimate sales volume, business will spend money to improve the productivity of office workers.

INFORMATION VENDING

Video entertainment has its counterpart in the office — what we call information vending. The value of information is highly dependent on how it's packaged and how quickly and easily it can be obtained. The coming electronic dissemination of information will enhance its accessibility, and therefore, increase its usefulness and value to the subscriber.

For example, the information in a business magazine might be worth as much as one hundred times its annual subscription price — if users could get the specific information they wanted electronically. So far, the business-information industry has grown at a rate of 20 percent a year, which is not surprising, because the business community has a virtually insatiable desire for relevant, timely information to assist in the decision-making process.

FACTORY ELECTRONICS

Some 600,000 commercial farmers presently produce nearly four times as much food as 6 million farmers did at the outbreak of World War II. The reason for this giant burst in productivity is capital investment. Since 1940 the capital investment behind every farm worker has jumped nearly tenfold. The same capital investment boom that has occurred on the farm will soon revolutionize our factories.

Several influences are at work which could encourage the trend toward factory automation accelerates, no matter what happens to capital spending as a whole. For one thing, many basic manufacturing industries have little choice — they must improve productivity by automating or they'll be forced out of business. What's more, low-cost, very powerful microcomputers have been around long enough to penetrate even the sleepy machinery and electrical equipment business. Finally, by 1984, the end of the baby boom will cause a sharp drop in the number of new entrants into the labor force, which will reduce the available supply of unskilled labor and encourage the trend toward automation.

DEREGULATION OF TRANSPORTATION

The deregulation of the nation's transportation system is producing dramatic change, as all deregulation does. A host of new products and services — everything from new commuter airlines to overnight delivery of packages — are bringing down the cost of transportation. These volume opportunities are being seized by select airline, trucking, and air freight companies that pick up market share from undercapitalized, inefficient businesses that can't compete well in this era of deregulation and high energy costs.

ENERGY PRODUCERS

In 1981 the twenty largest oil companies in the world (most of which are U.S.) spent only 20 percent of all the money expended on oil and natural gas exploration in the United States. The other 80 percent was spent by hundreds of small independent exploration companies that most people have never even heard of.

Success in discovering new reserves of oil and gas is directly related to how much money is spent looking for it. Accordingly, there is a massive market shift going on in the domestic energy industry. The big oil companies are investing a lot of money in non-energy businesses, such as minerals, electrical equipment, and food retailing.

Meanwhile, the need to discover domestic reserves of oil and gas should not be forgotten. According to industry estimates, U.S. oil and natural gas production from existing reservoirs is likely to fall by 40 percent or more in the 1980s.

ENERGY SERVICES

By 1990 the finders and producers of new reserves could receive between $200 and $300 billion in revenues per year. The development of this huge revenue stream is going to require continued capital investment in drilling rigs, drill bits, drilling fluids, and the many other accoutrements of the industry. Furthermore, as the trend toward deep drilling accelerates (because all the easy-to-find oil and gas has already been discovered), more sophisticated equipment and services will be required. Thus, the value of such services to the oil drilling industry should increase faster than the amount of actual drilling footage or drilling activity.

HEALTH CARE

The cost of hospital care in the United States has escalated far faster than the general rate of inflation. The Reagan administration's solution to this problem is to encourage for-profit hospital chains to help control costs. The volume opportunities become apparent since only some 15 percent of the $100 billion spent annually on hospital care goes to the privately owned chains. Free enterprise and professional management techniques are also being introduced to clinical laboratories and psychiatric hospitals.

Although most people think of biotechnology as exotic, it should be regarded as a cost-reducing innovation that will be an aid in finding new drug therapies.

SPECIALTY RETAILING

Major shifts in life styles and the way people spend their money have caused a major change in retailing. For one thing, the consumer wants a bigger selection to choose from and thus prefers to shop at specialty retailers where such a choice exists. What's more, faster economic growth in certain parts of the country favors those retailers who have a dominant position in such areas. Retail sales in the east- and south-central and west south-central regions will probably grow at 1.5 to 2 times the national average, offering good volume opportunities to certain retailers.

A number of companies are well situated to benefit from the trends in each of these ten industries discussed above. We believe that some of the companies in these industries may eventually become the IBMs and Xeroxes of the 1980s and 1990s. However, it's important to realize that the prime beneficiaries of these trends may not be the obvious ones. The producers of a certain type of productivity-related equipment may experience rapid growth accompanied by intense competition and an unexciting return. Take, as an example, the unexceptional profitability of all but a few of the semiconductor companies in the late 1970s. The company that most creatively employs the new product may end up being the real beneficiary.

While this book is largely about investing, it is also written for the entrepreneur, the businessman or woman, and the consumer. If we are correct in our forecasts, hundreds of thousands of new business opportunities will be found in these ten growth industries, and an explosion in new information in the office and new entertainment in

the home will affect almost every one of us, even if we're not entrepreneurs or investors.

But before we get more deeply into the specifics, we would like to
tell you why we think our economic problems may gradually begin
to recede in the years ahead.

CHAPTER 2

A Gradual Return to Economic Stability

If a committee of experts had sat down in January 1968 to write a blueprint for the devastation of the U.S. economic and social fabric, their policy prescriptions might have looked like this: "First, put the finishing touches on legislation that causes a massive redistribution of wealth. Second, escalate an increasingly unpopular war and then have the President who started it fail to run for reelection. Next, arrange the assassinations of two highly visible leaders, one white, one black. Then, devalue the dollar, close the gold window, impose a wage and price freeze, and allow the money supply to explode. Throw in a drought that doubles or triples the price of grain and remove the two top leaders of the country because their dishonesty is exposed. Finally, raise the price of the world's most important commodity, oil, from $2 a barrel to over $35."

Unfortunately, the economic and social events since 1968 could hardly have been more disruptive even if they had actually been planned that way. After the dramatic shocks of the 1970s and the 1980–82 recession, confidence can return only slowly and hesitatingly. There are bound to be frequent disappointments and the road back to stability may be a long and arduous one. Nevertheless, we believe that our economy is entering a much more positive environment than that of the 1970s. A number of important economic, demographic, and political factors are presently at work, which, taken together, could usher in a gradual improvement in our economy.

RETURN OF ENERGY PRICE STABILITY

The first positive factor is that energy prices, which disrupted the economy twice during the 1970s, are likely to remain stable during the 1980s. The Organization of Oil Exporting Countries' (OPEC) stranglehold on pricing began to weaken in 1980 because its $34-a-barrel price caused oil demand to slow, created the incentive for big increases in non-OPEC production, and pushed world economies farther down the road toward substitution.

Table 1 shows our forecast for the supply and demand of energy through 1990. As you can see, we expect natural gas, coal, and nuclear power to become increasingly important sources of energy. At the same time, non-OPEC oil production could increase from 21 million barrels a day in 1980 to an estimated 24 million barrels a day in 1990.

Table 1

WORLD ENERGY OUTLOOK

(All figures except OPEC price in millions of barrels per day of oil equivalent)

	1979	1980	1985	1990
Average OPEC price				
(1981 dollars per barrel)	22	34	40	48
World energy demand, outside Communist areas				
United States	37	36	37	40
Other industrial countries	43	43	46	50
Oil-exporting LDCs[a]	4	5	7	10
Other LDCs	11	11	12	14
Total	94	94	102	114
Energy supply				
Coal	17	18	21	25
Natural gas	16	17	20	22
Shale / heavy oil	—	—	—	1
Nuclear	3	3	5	9
Hydro / other	7	7	8	10
Communist exports	2	2	2	2
Subtotal	45	46	56	69
Oil Required from non-Communist areas	50	48	46	45
Non-OPEC production	20	21	23	24
OPEC production	31	27	23	21

[a] Less developed countries.

As the economy recovers, worldwide demand for energy should increase by the equivalent of 20 million barrels a day over the course of the 1980s. That increased demand will be more than met by non-OPEC oil production and greater usage of coal, nuclear power, and natural gas. Thus, OPEC production will likely keep on dropping — from 31 million barrels a day in 1979 to 21 million in 1990. Indeed, during the 1982 recession, OPEC production dropped to below 18 million barrels a day, an indication of OPEC's diminished power.

There is always the risk of political unrest in the Middle East or of another oil embargo, but we think OPEC's declining share of energy production will provide a supply cushion that was not there during the 1970s. Furthermore, Saudi Arabia, which controls 25 percent of OPEC's producing capacity and owns one third of its oil reserves, is committed to a policy of price stability. Now that the Saudis have regained control over OPEC pricing, they will likely institute price hikes, if any, based on the economic growth, currency values, and inflation rates of the industrialized nations. Such a policy means that any future energy price increases are likely to be easily absorbed by our economy.

We think a 4 percent annual real oil price increase is about the best OPEC could achieve once the economy recovers. Real price increases of more than 4 percent would hasten substitution and a decline in demand for OPEC oil.

Most importantly, as shown in Exhibit 2–1, gradual increases in price of 4 percent a year would insure a reasonable balance between supply and demand. The shortages projected for the mid-1980s would be put off until 1995. Gradual price increases would encourage sufficient conservation, substitution, and higher non-OPEC production to avoid the supply disruptions of the 1970s.

If, in fact, the price of energy is more stable in the 1980s, an important element of the inflation of the 1970s will be reduced. Since almost every American consumer is affected by rising gasoline or heating oil prices, any moderation in their rise or actual price declines like those we experienced during 1982 would do a lot to boost consumer confidence and lower inflationary expectations.

Greater energy price stability would also be a positive factor for corporate America. A lot of time and resources have undoubtedly been diverted from the normal course of business to deal with the

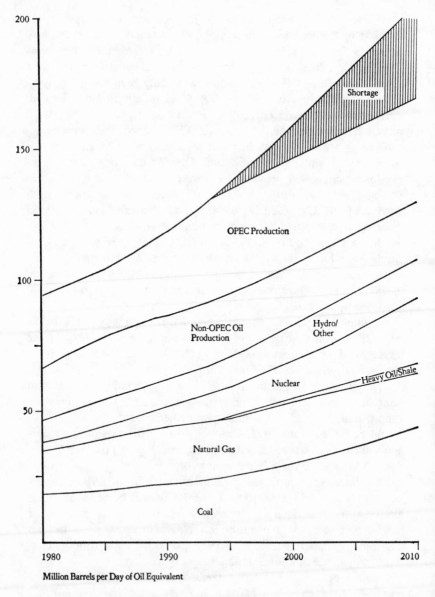

Million Barrels per Day of Oil Equivalent

Exhibit 2 – 1
Outlook for world energy supplies.

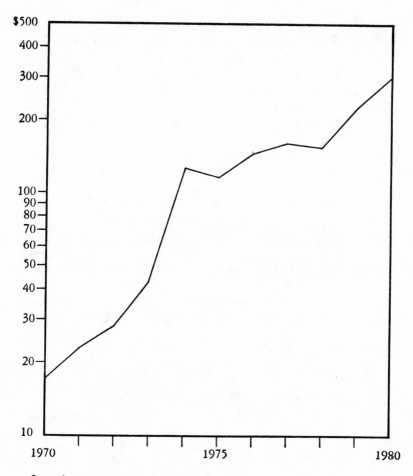

Source: International Monetary Fund.
1980 excludes Gabon.

Exhibit 2 – 2
OPEC revenues (in billions).

energy problem. If a measure of stability returns, corporate executives and resources could be free to pursue profits and growth.

Energy price stability could also reduce the difficulty of controlling our money supply. As is clear from Exhibit 2 – 2, OPEC oil exports rose from less than $20 billion in 1970 to $300 billion in 1980. Since most of these exports were denominated in U.S. dollars, it created a massive, uncontrolled market of offshore dollars. Although the problem of OPEC's impact on monetary policy isn't over, the rate of change should slow markedly.

TECHNOLOGY INVADES THE SERVICES SECTOR

The second positive development for the U.S. economy is the improving outlook for productivity as technology invades the service sector of the economy, which is where the greatest productivity problem lies. As you can see from Table 2, overall productivity in the economy slumped by one half a percentage point during the last five years of the 1970s as compared with the prior ten-year period. But interestingly, manufacturing productivity actually rose from 1.7

Table 2

PRODUCTIVITY IN U.S. ECONOMY

Industry	% 1964 – 1974	% 1974 – 1979	% 1985E	Estimated % of 1985 output
Manufacturing	+1.7	+2.7	+3.0	26.0
Trade	+2.4	+1.1	+2.0	21.0
Financial	+1.1	+0.4	+1.5	19.0
Services	+1.6	+0.3	+1.5	16.0
Transportation	+2.8	+0.5	+1.0	4.5
Communications	+4.4	+6.8	+7.0	5.0
Mining / contractors	−0.8	−1.6	−2.0	6.0
Utilities	+2.6	+0.7	+1.0	2.5
Total	+1.7	+1.3	+2.0	100.0

percent to 2.7 percent. The trade, financial, and services categories, which account for some 50 percent of our nonfarm business output and employ 50 million persons, show low or fading productivity gains in the late 1970s.

It is in these people-intensive areas that the introduction of automation at the individual level (word processors, local computer terminals for the input and retrieval of data, and personal computers) offers the greatest promise of improved productivity. As technology invades this part of the economy, we expect that overall productivity could jump to 2 percent a year by 1985.

The rationale for this type of capital investment is convincing. For one thing, the purchase of productivity-enhancing technology makes economic sense. Such equipment is usually amortized over one to three years, a modest cost, especially in comparison with a building or a conventional plant that may have a twenty to thirty-year payback.

A data processing investment of $2,500 for a service-sector employee would double the current per capita capital investment and buy a very substantial amount of computing power — enough to lead to a 10 percent productivity improvement for many employees. Assuming an average annual salary of $13,000, a 10 percent productivity improvement leads to a very attractive three-year after-tax investment payback. In the highly compensated professional segments of services, the economics can be several times more attractive, with an investment payback measured in months.

Spending $2,500 on 50 percent of the 50 million service sector employees, would amount to $70 billion in 1981 dollars. But the cost of these products per unit of performance is dropping at least 15 – 20 percent per year. Spread out over several years, the nominal dollar cost might well be only half of the $70 billion, or only several billion dollars per year, a very small fraction of total capital spending.

There is increasing evidence that the transformation in the efficiency of the services sector is already well under way. All of the copiers Xerox produces now have a communications capability. McGraw-Hill has begun to distribute some of its data services, heretofore available only as hard copy, over an electronics communications network. Dow Jones now offers its news and quotation services to owners of Apple personal computers. And Dun & Bradstreet has initiated electronic access to its financial information service.

The evidence of what's happening will mount with each passing year. Very broad based financial services, such as those being developed by Dow Jones, will become more and more available. Electronic mail will start to be used on a large scale. Professional use of personal computers will rise exponentially. And the number of data communication devices (such as terminals and video screens) sitting on office desks will rise significantly.

Perhaps the most important benefit of this type of capital investment is that its cost will continue to decline. As the base of installed technology grows, the proportion of our capital stock that is technology-related will increase. This means that the cost of replacing our capital stock over the years will start to decline — as opposed to the increases we have had to live with for the last decade. Imagine the benefit to the cash flow of a corporation that can replace a part of its capital base with a new piece of equipment that actually costs less than the old one or has significantly greater capabilities for the same price. Think also of the positive effect on the capital markets, which have been overwhelmed in recent years by the demand for credit.

FAVORABLE DEMOGRAPHIC TRENDS

The third positive development for the U.S. economy will be the boost given our productivity by some major improvements in demographic trends. Slowly but surely, the baby-boom generation is moving from being an expense and a drag on the economy to becoming an important contributor. Between 1947 and 1957 some 43 million babies were born; in 1981 they were aged between twenty-four and thirty-four and represented some 20 percent of our population. While growing up, this huge generation of babies had been a financial burden, for their parents and on society in general. The cost of food, clothes, and education were a major drain on family budgets. And later, as this group finished their education, the business community and the taxpayers underwrote the enormous cost of training them for gainful employment.

But by 1981 most of the group had been in the job force long enough to have mastered basic skills and were in a position to improve national productivity. In fact, a case could be made that these workers will improve productivity and raise total income as greatly as they squeezed them in the past.

The effect of this could be startling, especially if you put things in historical perspective. In 1950 there were roughly 1½ parents per child. But by 1970 some 26 percent of the population was being supported and reared by only 24 percent — in other words, less than one parent per child.

By 1985 the ratio of parents to children will be even more favorable than it was before the baby boom began. The group will span the thirty to forty-year age bracket, typically a period of great achievement, rapidly rising income, and realization of certain work goals. Also, as the generation attains financial self-sufficiency, the burden of education and support will drop sharply.

FAVORABLE GOVERNMENT ECONOMIC POLICY
FOR PRIVATE ENTERPRISE

The fourth and perhaps the most favorable development of all for the U.S. economy is a significant shift in government economic pol-

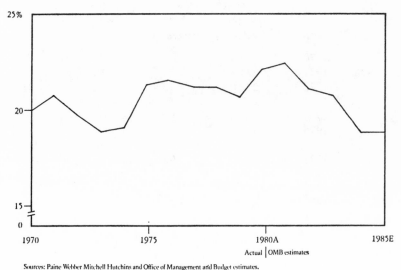

Sources: Paine Webber Mitchell Hutchins and Office of Management and Budget estimates.

Exhibit 2 – 3
Federal spending as percent of nominal GNP.

icy. The major aim of the new shift is to alter the relative attractiveness of work versus leisure and savings versus consumption and to encourage economic growth. The government's strategy is being implemented on three levels: attempts to get control over government spending, deregulation of the private sector, and changes in the tax code.

To bring government spending under control will be a difficult battle, but the Reagan administration is apparently committed to reducing federal spending as a percent of GNP. Exhibit 2–3 shows how the Administration proposes to lower the government's share of GNP from 22.4 percent in fiscal 1981 to 18.8 percent in fiscal 1985. As you can see from Table 3, real spending is scheduled to increase at a slower rate than at any time since 1970.

Table 3

FEDERAL SPENDING

Fiscal year	Federal spending ($ billions)	% increase	% real increases
1970	196.6	—	—
1971	221.4	7.5	2.5
1972	232.0	11.0	6.8
1973	247.1	6.5	0.8
1974	269.6	9.1	0.4
1975	326.2	21.0	11.7
1976	366.4	12.3	7.1
1977	402.7	9.9	4.1
1978	450.8	11.9	4.6
1979	493.6	9.5	1.0
1980	579.6	17.4	8.4
1981	662.0	14.2	1.6
1982E	695.5	6.2	−1.8
1983E	733.1	5.4	−1.1
1984E	771.6	5.2	0.2
1985E	844.0	9.4	4.9

If President Reagan succeeds in reducing federal spending as a percentage of GNP to 18.8 percent in fiscal 1985, we estimate that the private sector would grow 1.5 percent faster than if federal spending remained at current levels of GNP.

The impact of government deregulation on the U.S. economy is even more positive. The unintended negative consequences of regulations are widespread, and removing the more onerous ones could reduce costs and improve business problem-solving ability.

For instance, a study in the mid-1970s found that 43 percent of chief executive officers surveyed spent at least 25 percent of their time on regulatory matters. Or take the typical U.S.-manufactured auto of 1978, which carried some $666 worth of government-mandated safety and pollution equipment, representing nearly 10 percent of the car's purchase price. Or consider the famous story about the federally mandated noise-control standards that would cost the steel industry $1.2 million per affected worker — an expenditure easily replaced by a $10 set of ear protectors. The removal of even a part of this time-and-cost burden can only be a very positive development for business.

Another plus, as we see it, is the government's trend toward encouraging competition in many sectors of the economy. Five major industries that account for some 50 percent of GNP — health care, financial services, telecommunications, transportation, and energy — are being deregulated.

Consider the recent developments in the transportation industry, which has been in a period of deregulation for several years and where firms such as Air Florida, New York Air, and People Express offer services at prices well below the competition. While deregulation is not a one-way street and many weaker companies will suffer, the end result will be lower prices for the consumer and more productive employment of labor and capital.

The most controversial of all the new government policies is the three-year cut in tax rates. It is the Administration's hope that by lowering tax rates, people will view work as more appealing than leisure, and investment and savings as more appealing than spending.

It seems clear that some sort of tax relief was necessary. Our federal tax code was designed for a noninflationary economy, and the inflation of recent years has pushed everyone into ever-higher tax brackets. If taxes weren't too high, then why have tens of billions of dollars a year flowed into tax shelters? Why does the United States have the lowest savings rate in the industrialized world? Why did California's Proposition 13 occur? Why is the underground, or off-the-books, economy exploding?

While many people fundamentally favor reducing taxes, they worry that a tax cut is inflationary and will add to an already overwhelming federal deficit. They reason thus: tax cuts will increase the federal deficit, boost interest rates, and give consumers more money to spend, which will "stimulate" the economy and demand, thereby fueling inflation.

Not only do supporters of lower taxes argue that this reasoning is faulty, but they also believe that a cut in tax rates might eventually reduce inflation. To be sure, for all the inflation scare talk generated by President Reagan's program, no one has yet to answer his question: why is it that when government spends your money, it's not inflationary, but when you spend it, it is?

In fact, some economists argue that high taxes are inflationary. Colin Clark, in a paper published after World War II by the Institute of Economic Affairs in London, concludes as follows:

"Taxation . . . raises costs partly through discouraging productive effort; more significantly, perhaps, in causing industrialists to become careless about costs (if half of any increase in costs is 'on the Treasury,' they will make much less effort to avoid it, whether it be a wage increase, interest charges, or an expense account) and, finally and in rather a subtle manner, the existence of a high level of taxation alters the whole climate of politics: politicians tend to lose their capacity to resist pressures, whether governmental or private, leading to cost increases, in the more or less unconscious knowledge that a rise in prices will lower the real value of all fixed charges on the budget and in that way lighten their burden."*

Clark believed that when taxation exceeds 25 percent of net national income (and he included the government deficit in his calcu-

* Colin Clark, *Taxmanship: Principles and Proposals for the Reform of Taxation*, Hobart Paper 26, Institute of Economic Affairs Ltd., London, 1964, p. 23.

lations), the stage was set for a rise in costs and prices within the ensuing two-to-three-year period.

Even Lord Keynes, the father of postwar economic policies, agreed with this view; in a personal letter to Clark, dated May 1, 1944, Keynes made the following amazing admission: "I should guess that your figure of 25 percent on the maximum tolerable proportion of taxation may be exceedingly near the truth. I should not be at all surprised if we did not find further confirmation in our post-war experience of your empirical law." Clark delighted in quoting Keynes himself as a rebuttal to the many economists who incorrectly cited Keynes as a major advocate of unlimited taxation.

A RETURN TO DISCIPLINE IN MONETARY POLICY

Many lay persons these days have become experts on monetary policy, as evidenced by the attention paid to the weekly money supply figures released by the Federal Reserve every Friday at 4:00 P.M. EST. Given the close correlation between money supply growth and inflation, this obsession with the weekly figures is not as overdone as one might think.

In any event, the outlook for a stable monetary policy has improved. First, Congress and the White House are not likely to interfere with Federal Reserve policy as much as in the past. For most of the 1970s, stable interest rates were preferred over a stable dollar, and the inflation problem was left for another day. But starting in the latter days of the Carter administration, this attitude seems to have changed. The White House has several competent Fed watchers on its staff, and there appears to be continued support for a gradual slowing in money growth.

Tight monetary policy has historically conflicted with the so-called core rate of inflation, causing interest rates to surge and the real economy to sink without any significant change in the course of inflation. Indeed, the multiple trips to very high interest rates in recent years are prime examples of this. Ultimate success in monetary policy depends upon whether the core rate of inflation, as represented by labor contracts and other pricing arrangements, can be changed. We think there's cause for optimism. At Chrysler, General Motors, Ford, Firestone, and U. S. Steel, there have already been reductions in labor cost settlements and Conrail is attempting to obtain a substantial reduction in labor contract terms. While wage concessions to date are not large in total dollars, they have been coming in the right places: to companies and industries in poor competitive positions.

Finally, as we discussed above, the Fed's time-honored enemy — profligate federal spending — seems headed in a positive direction. The continued pressure of high interest rates will inevitably force spending reductions to help narrow the deficit. It is important that the deficits planned between fiscal 1981 and fiscal 1984 are not being created to "prime the pump" or to encourage an economic up-cycle, but rather to provide for new tax-based incentives at the cost of an immediate reduction in the deficit. Hence, there is no overt pressure on the Fed to monetize these deficits.

The progress in 1981 in slowing the growth of the money supply is encouraging. As can be seen from Table 4, the average annual increase in the monetary base throughout the 1970s was 8 percent. In 1981 the monetary base grew at scarcely more than half that rate.

Table 4

ADJUSTED MONETARY BASE

	Yearly average ($ billions)	% increase	% nominal GNP	% real growth	% deflator
1970	72.183	4.9	5.2	−0.2	5.4
1971	77.883	7.9	8.6	3.4	5.0
1972	83.608	7.4	10.1	5.7	4.2
1973	90.433	8.2	11.8	5.8	5.7
1974	97.933	8.3	8.1	−0.6	8.7
1975	105.358	7.6	8.0	−1.1	9.3
1976	113.317	7.6	10.9	5.4	5.2
1977	122.500	8.1	11.6	5.5	5.8
1978	133.858	9.3	12.4	4.8	7.3
1979	144.958	8.3	12.0	3.2	8.5
1980	156.600	8.0	8.8	−0.2	9.0
1981	164.000	4.7	11.1	2.0	9.1

REASSERTION OF U.S. PRESENCE IN THE WORLD

The decade of the 1970s was an era of retreat for the United States, and the stability we had offered the world for most of the postwar period appeared to be irrevocably lost. But the humiliation of the U.S. Embassy hostages in Iran, the Soviet invasion of Afghanistan, and the obvious vulnerability of the United States to any crisis in the oil fields of the Middle East have caused a major shift in national policy toward defense spending.

President Reagan is clearly committed to a major buildup in our defense system, as you can see from Table 5. These figures are only estimates and increases in defense spending will undoubtedly be reduced as pressure mounts to cut the deficit, but the trend will continue upward.

Table 5

U.S. DEFENSE SPENDING

Year	Federal budget ($ billions)	% change	% GNP deflator	% real change
1971	75,808	—	—	—
1972	76,550	+1.0	4.2	−3.2
1973	74,541	−2.6	5.7	−8.3
1974	77,781	+4.3	8.7	−4.4
1975	85,552	+10.0	9.3	+0.7
1976	89,430	+4.5	5.2	−0.7
1977	97,501	+9.0	5.8	+3.2
1978	105,186	+7.9	7.3	+0.6
1979	117,681	+11.9	8.5	+3.4
1980	135,856	+15.3	9.0	+6.3
1981	159,500	+17.4	9.0	+8.4
1982E	188,800	+18.1	8.0	+10.1
1983E	226,900	+20.2	6.5	+13.7
1984E	255,600	+12.6	5.0	+7.6
1985E	295,000	+15.4	4.5	+10.9

A reassertion of the U.S. presence abroad will eventually be a positive development for world trade, as well as an important psychological plus for the financial markets.

THE BENEFIT TO COMMON STOCKS OF A BALANCED ECONOMY

The economic scenario that we have presented here would unquestionably be positive for the stock markets, since economic growth and improving confidence would go a long way toward restoring common stocks to investor favor.

One method of evaluating the relative value of stocks is to look at the relationship between stock prices and earnings — the price / earnings, or p / e, ratio. This is also one of the best measures of investor confidence. If p / e ratios are at historic highs, it means that investors put a big value on present and future earnings, which suggests long-term confidence. Conversely, if p / e ratios are abnormally depressed, as they are at present, it is a reflection of great uncertainty.

There also appears to be a close correlation between p / e ratios and real economic growth. As shown in Exhibit 2 – 4, real growth in gross national product began to slow around 1970, and dividends of the S&P 500 (Standard & Poor's average of five hundred large industrial companies) followed a few years later. We think it is no coincidence that p / e ratios subsequently declined.

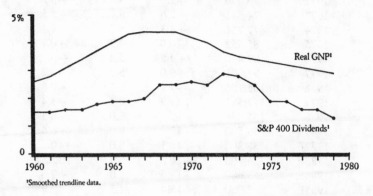

¹Smoothed trendline data.

Exhibit 2 – 4
Real growth of S&P 500 dividends and the GNP.

In fact, a good case can be made that the prospect of a drop in real economic growth was the main factor behind the erosion of p / e ratios. If so, then rising real economic growth might cause p / e ratios to double from the 7 – 8 level of today to the 15 – 20 level, which prevailed for much of the 1958 – 72 period. Exhibit 2 – 5 shows the p / e ratios for the S&P 400 (Standard & Poor's average of four hundred large industrial companies) since 1950. As you can see, p / e ratios gradually increased throughout the 1950s, remained in a trading range throughout the 1960s, and then plummeted in the 1970s. After the 1980 – 82 market decline runs its course, p / e ratios should begin a gradual recovery.

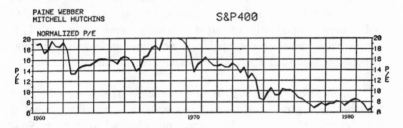

Exhibit 2 – 5
Price / earnings ratio of S&P 400 stock average.

CONTRARY THINKING: IS INFLATION DEAD?

Disinflation and economic stability may be difficult for most of us to accept. The shocks of which we spoke at the beginning of this chapter are still very much with us. And a majority of people believe that it is not stability that's just around the corner, but rather runaway inflation.

Those familiar with the art of contrary thinking know that the consensus is rarely right on economic and investment matters. By the late 1920s, economists expected the boom to last forever. Later, after World War II, the majority of forecasters feared a return to depression, while in reality, we began the longest period of economic boom in our country's history.

But by 1973 prosperity was so firmly ingrained in our psyche that economists predicted that the business cycle had been repealed. Yes, they said, the all-powerful, all-encompassing government, with its magical fiscal and monetary tools, could effectively smooth out the ups and downs that had plagued economies since the start of the Industrial Revolution. In 1981 we still remember some of the most notable of our most notable economists' predictions in 1974: "A soft landing in the valley of the dulls"; "the recession we almost had is almost over"; "this is no recession, merely 'an oil spasm.'" As you may recall, shortly thereafter, we entered the severest recession since the 1930s.

Since the pundits erred by not anticipating the 1974–75 recession, they apparently resolved to be on top of the next one. Accordingly, after only a couple years of expansion, widespread forecasts of recession began to hit the business weeklies. To be sure, throughout 1978 and 1979 a majority of economists, as well as those most professionally optimistic of all forecasters, government officials, agreed that we were on the brink of a downturn in business. But the economy confounded them all by expanding during the entire period.

Then, in December 1979, out of the blue, the Soviets invaded Afghanistan and the world was faced with the possibility of a hot war. Sentiment about the U.S. economy changed overnight. Suddenly everyone agreed that there wouldn't be a recession after all. Defense spending would have to be boosted sharply, which would keep the economy rolling along indefinitely, or so said the pundits. This shift in sentiment, ironically, came at just about the time that the recession began in earnest.

The same pattern of miscalculation appears in the investment world. The classic example is a 129-page book entitled *Common Stocks as Long Term Investments* by Edgar Lawrence Smith, which was published in 1924. Smith was an economist and investment analyst who had studied the record of bonds, stocks, and commodities from the end of the Civil War to 1923 and had come to the revolutionary conclusion that stocks, not bonds, were the best long-term investments.

As commonplace as that may sound to us now, it represented a 180-degree reversal of the conventional wisdom of the time. Stocks were generally regarded as good speculations, but certainly not good long-term investments. Bonds, on the other hand, were considered an excellent place to put your capital for the long haul.

Smith's thesis attracted a lot of attention, and in the years

1924 – 29, a host of Wall Street brokers carried his message to millions of Americans. But in an amazing example of irony, his book did not become a best seller until 1929. When you consider that the Dow plunged from its high of nearly 400 in 1929 to around 40 in 1932, the popularity of the book has to go down as one of the worst instances of investment timing on record.

Other best-selling investment books have proven equally ill-timed. The seventh best-selling nonfiction book in 1968 was Adam Smith's *The Money Game,* which was essentially about speculating in the stock market. As it turned out, 1968 — the very year that the public pushed the book onto the best-seller list — marked the end of the great postwar bull market in stocks.

The seventh nonfiction best seller in 1974 was *You Can Profit from a Monetary Crisis,* by Harry Browne. Nineteen seventy-four was the year the price of gold peaked at $197 an ounce, then plummeting to $103 by the middle of 1976 and dragging down gold shares to a small fraction of their former highs.

More recently, three investment books have broken all records. Howard Ruff's *How to Prosper During the Coming Bad Years* reportedly had the largest paperback sale of any financial book on record. Douglas Casey's *Crisis Investing: Opportunities and Profits in the Coming Great Depression* became the number one hardcover nonfiction best seller for all of 1981 — the first time a money book ever did so well. And early in 1981 Jerome Smith's *The Coming Currency Collapse* inched its way up as high as the number three position on the New York *Times* best-seller list.

The last three books were launched with huge advertising budgets, much to-do, and fanfare. Major newspapers around the country were blanketed with full-page advertisements announcing that hyperinflation was around the corner.

We've never had three investment best sellers harping on the same theme before. If sheer volume means anything (and it does), the forecasts of hyperinflation may prove remarkably ill-timed. Let's recap the record discussed above. One best-selling book on the stock market coincided with the worst crash in stock market history; another one became popular on the eve of the worst bear market since the great depression; and a 1974 book on gold ushered in a 50 percent drop in the price of bullion.

One can't help but wonder if inflation is finally dead. Indeed, if there is anything to worry about, it is deflation, not a quick revival of inflation.

Economists and investment experts often overlook the importance of psychology in economic revival. A return of confidence and hope, or in this case, an overwhelming victory over inflation, can sometimes produce seemingly impossible results.

Consider the experience in Germany after World War II. West German Economic Minister Ludwig Erhard, in his 1958 book *Prosperity Through Competition,* describes the economic environment after the war as a time when "it was calculated that for every German there would be one plate every five years, a pair of shoes every twelve years, a suit every fifty years; that only every fifth infant would lie in its own napkins and that only every third German would have a chance of being buried in his own coffin."

Erhard proposed a simple cure for the German economy, which in the mid-to-late 1940s had "returned to a state of primitive barter." He felt that the solution lay "in multiplying the national income"— rather than in trying to slice it up. Incentive and growth were encouraged.

"New stimuli for investment were continually being offered," wrote Erhard, "and extra effort was encouraged because overtime payments remained tax-free. The joy of working, so recently regained, now meant so much more since wages at last had purchasing power again. . . ."

What was the net result of Erhard's policies? An unparalleled economic expansion: the cost-of-living index of a working class family of four people fell from 166 in the last quarter of 1948 (1936=100) to 149 in July 1950; gross national income soared from 47.9 billion deutsche marks (in 1936 prices) in 1949 to DM 85.8 billion in 1955. All this economic growth and prosperity allowed social benefits to increase from DM 9.6 billion in 1949 to DM 21 billion in 1955.

Perhaps the best commentary on the dramatic change that took place in Germany's economy after economic freedom was restored was made by Jacques Rueff and André Piettre:

"If the state of recovery [in West Germany] was a surprise, its swiftness was even more so . . . On the eve of currency reform the

Germans were aimlessly wandering about their towns in search of a few additional items of food. A day later they thought of nothing but producing them. One day apathy was mirrored on their faces while on the next a whole nation looked hopefully into the future."*

* In Ludwig Erhard, *Prosperity Through Competition*, p. 3.

CHAPTER 3

Relative Price Investing and the New Great Growth Companies

Vision has a lot to do with success. Being able to discern the future or to determine correctly that certain things will occur gives one a decided advantage in the competition of life. By the same token, almost every successful investor has a vision of the future, a modus operandi, a plan, a long-term strategy, or a judgment about how events will unfold. Such a system goes by many names, but it is essential to continued success.

This book is based on a very definite strategy, one that, to our knowledge, has not been suggested or used elsewhere. In this sense, it is an original investment plan for the rest of the 1980s.

Our thesis, simply stated, is that we are in an era of profound relative price change, more profound than anything seen in decades — a change that will have dramatic and long-lasting impact on almost every industry in America.

THE MEANING OF RELATIVE PRICE CHANGE

By "relative price change," we are not referring to price inflation as measured by the consumer price index (CPI), but rather to the individual prices of hundreds of essentials within the economy. Although it may come as a surprise to most people, there has been little consistency in price changes between most items in the economy.

Between 1975 and 1979, for instance, when the rate of inflation averaged 8 – 9 percent, price increases of many items were either well above that rate or well below it. Some specific annual price increases during that period were 29 percent for natural gas, 19 percent for gasoline, 11.2 percent for shoes, 9.7 percent for tires, 9.5 percent for medical care, 6.9 percent for automobiles, 6.5 percent for furniture, 5.4 percent for paint, 5.3 percent for appliances, 4.8 percent for home furnishings, 4.6 percent for fresh fruits, 4 percent for apparel. At the same time there was a decline of 1.5 percent for electronics and 2.1 percent for chicken. Hardly a homogeneous price movement.

Perhaps the greatest example of relative price change lies in the changing differential between energy and technology as shown in Exhibit 3 – 1. The cost of one MIP (a computer that can process 1 million instructions per second) has gone from 3.5 million barrels of oil in the early 1970s to 13,000 at present. That shift represents a 260-fold change in relative price in less than a decade.

Consumers and business people alike recognize the importance of relative price. Hardly a day goes by when we don't make a decision based on relative value. The price of beef goes up, so the housewife shifts to lower priced chicken. The price of gasoline skyrockets and small, energy-efficient cars become the latest thing. A glut of oil forces gasoline prices lower, and the gasoline station with the biggest discount gets most of the local business. Regional airlines cut their fares, and their business booms.

By the same token, the demand for various products or services within the economy might shift because of changing buyer preferences. For example, the percentage of consumer spending going for food has dropped from 23 percent in 1960 to 17 percent today. This means an estimated $120 billion annually is being spent somewhere else in the economy.

The trade-off between work and leisure and between consuming and saving that we mentioned in the last chapter is another example of relative "price," or relative value. If taxes are lowered enough, work and the ability to earn more money become more attractive. If incentives for savings are increased enough, consuming what one earns may not be so appealing.

In fact, one could argue that everything is relative. The stock market is only attractive relative to competing investments, such as interest rates. A given rate of inflation is high or low, depending on where you live. In West Germany inflation is only the tiniest fraction of that in Argentina. Alternatively, economic growth may be high or

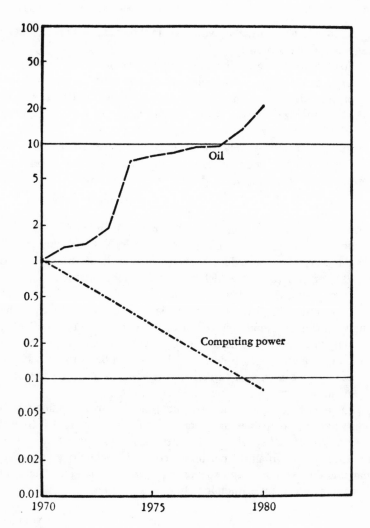

Exhibit 3 – 1
Relative price change of oil and computing power.

low, depending on whether you live in booming South Korea or stagnating Great Britain.

What we are trying to illustrate here is that the relatively high or low price of a product, commodity, or service will have a great bearing on final demand. Consumers, business people, and investors all quickly recognize relative price changes and alter their spending priorities accordingly.

If prices remain relatively low or actually decline, volume may expand, which in turn could create a good business and investment opportunity. On the other hand, if prices were to rise because of shortages, a product or commodity sold by a company might increase a lot in value.

As anyone familiar with business knows, there are three basic ways to increase profits—you can increase sales volume (that is, sell more units); you can reduce costs (bringing all of the savings to profits); or you can get a higher price for your product, assuming your costs increase at a slower rate than your prices.

Of the three, the best way to increase business profits over the long term is greater unit volume, particularly in a time of disinflation. Not only does more volume permit lower costs through efficiencies of scale, but it increases cash flow, which can then be reinvested in the business so it can expand further or cut costs through the purchase of the latest productivity-enhancing technology.

The goal of a successful investment strategy is to determine which industries and companies are likely to register substantial increases in sales volume. We believe that there are four basic factors that influence sales volume: declining cost of technology; scarcity; changing demographics and spending patterns of the consumer; and changing government economic policy.

Any reduction in relative price of a product can increase volume, but the most interesting and pervasive example at the moment is electronics technology. Exhibit 3 – 2 is a pyramid depicting our view of how declining costs have broadened the market and the volume opportunities for technology. The top of the pyramid was the market in the 1950s. But, with each drop in the cost of technology the market increased. The greatest volume opportunities now lie ahead.

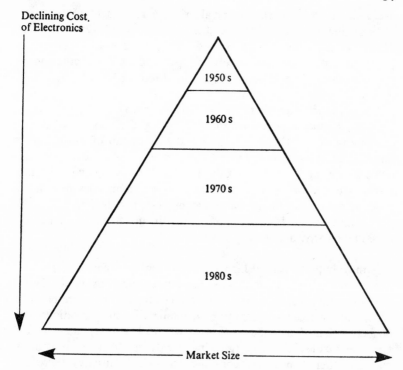

Exhibit 3 – 2
Volume opportunities in technology.

We expect technology to enter our economy through three broad markets: the home (i.e., the individual consumer), the office, and the factory. The ultimate impact in these areas is so potentially revolutionary that it cannot be fully comprehended at this time.

From our vantage point at the present, we see enormous volume opportunities in personal automation hardware, video entertainment, office automation, information vending, and factory electronics.

The second impetus behind higher sales volume is a shortage of an item, product, or commodity. Consider what happened to commercial real estate in New York City. Construction of new office space in Manhattan virtually stopped in the mid-1970s because of overbuilding, New York's financial crisis, a movement of corporations to the suburbs and the Sunbelt, and the 1974 – 75 recession. When the economy picked up and foreigners started investing in New York, a shortage of space developed and rents for prime midtown locations jumped from $10 a square foot in 1975 to over $40 by 1981.

A much more damaging shortage was energy. Domestic price controls, minuscule domestic exploration, rising demand, and the increasing power of OPEC all combined to push up oil prices some thirteenfold in less than a decade. But just as owners and builders of office space in New York City benefited from tightness in the market, so the energy producers and service companies now have good volume opportunities at these higher price levels. While oil prices have dropped recently, they are still much higher than they were in the early to middle 1970s.

A third impetus behind higher sales volume is a changing perception among consumers as to what constitutes value, or good relative price. If certain parts of the United States attract consumers because of climate or economic opportunity, retailers in those locations will do better than their counterparts elsewhere. Likewise, sales of certain merchandise that suits growing trends in life-style preferences may do better than overall consumer sales. In both cases, there are good opportunities for increasing volume.

The fourth cause of higher sales volume is a major change in government economic policy. We have spoken earlier of tax legislation that aims to make consumption less attractive than savings and leisure less attractive than work. We have also spoken of government deregulation, which is creating volume opportunities for strongly capitalized, innovative firms. We think the volume possibilities in the transportation industry are particularly interesting.

But there is another side to every volume opportunity, as you can see from Exhibit 3 – 3. The high price of energy has hurt the automobile and chemical industries as well as electric utilities; it has also weakened the competitive position of many airlines, truckers, and airfreight companies. Other industries are squeezed by changing consumption patterns or preferences for new products or services, such as video entertainment. The industries being squeezed are housing, retailing in general, cosmetics / toiletries, household products, photography, appliances, and conventional leisure businesses. Other industries that are not directly affected, but will probably lose out on a relative basis because the volume opportunities that will be elsewhere are paper / forest products, steel, packaging, and tobacco.

Beneficiaries of cheap technology:	Entertainment Factory Electronics	Office Automation Personal Technology	Personal Automation Information Vending
Changing consumption patterns:	Specialty Retailing Health Care		
The squeezed:	Autos Chemicals Airlines Air Freight Truckers Electric Utilities Housing Retailing Cosmetics/Toiletries	Household Products Photography Appliances	Conventional Leisure Durables
No major effect:	Paper/Forest Products Gaming/Lodging	Financial Ethical Drugs Steel	Packaging Aerospace Tobacco
Changing government rules:	Transportation		
Beneficiaries of high resource prices:	Natural Gas	Energy Services	Railroads

Exhibit 3 – 3
Industry overview for 1980s.

As we think back over the great growth companies of the past, we can see that the growth of almost every one has been stimulated by changes in relative prices. Here are a few examples that come to mind: IBM grew rapidly throughout the postwar period because it constantly lowered the cost of computing power. Drug chains achieved excellent rates of growth by underselling local drug stores. McDonald's achieved its record by making eating out inexpensive and accessible to almost everyone. Black & Decker popularized home repair by lowering the cost of electric tools. The mass production of the automobile brought about such reductions in unit costs that almost anyone could afford a car (at least, until changes in the relative price of energy and labor altered the picture). The introduction of low-cost copying enabled Xerox to record exceptional growth in the 1960s. Some companies even grew by selling a better product at the same price, for instance, manufacturers of color TV sets in the 1960s.

CHAPTER 4

Personal Automation Hardware

It used to be that only one generation in many was lucky enough to actually watch a revolution unfold before their very eyes, but the last hundred years have been different. Those born around the turn of the century grew up with the mass production of the automobile, which brought about a revolution in transportation and individual independence. Later, in the 1950s and early 1960s, a host of household appliances (the clothes dryer, the dishwasher, the food blender, and such) invaded the home, all of them generally aimed at improving the productivity of the housewife.

The next revolution is taking place right now in electronics, and in many ways it's the most exciting event for consumers in many decades. By 1990 we expect electronics to revolutionize the home.

The real benefit to consumers will be an explosion in the amount of available electronic entertainment. Up until now, most of us have been confined to the dismal alternatives of the three major TV networks. Unfortunately, unless about 15 million people tune in to a show during prime time, the network soon cancels the program. Why? Well, the greater the audience for a show, the more the network can charge the sponsor or commercial advertiser.

With the new technologies, the choices of entertainment will be numerous. For instance, cable TV (CATV) systems with as many as 120 different channels will soon become available. That means a particular show, sporting event, concert, or documentary that can only garner a minuscule audience might become economically viable to owners of cable TV systems.

Think of some of the events and entertainment that might one day be available on your TV screen: every major or minor sporting event in the country; films; documentaries; contests such as the world chess championship; stage plays; opera performances; in-depth financial and business news; and talk shows or specials on every topic of human interest you can imagine, from great literature to the lives of famous people to nutrition to jogging tips to artificial respiration.

But best of all, new technologies such as videocassette recorders (VCRs) and videodisc players will allow you to watch this enter-tainment when you want. Perhaps you're away on a business trip and can't watch an important baseball or football game, or maybe you have a social engagement on the same night an old movie you've been wanting to see for years is to be broadcast. Videocas-sette recorders, with their ability to record TV programming, can eliminate such problems for you.

By 1990 the TV set will have been transformed from a passive to an active appliance. It will be the centerpiece of most of the hard-ware items in the home — the videocassette recorder, the videodisc player, video games, and the personal computer all will use the TV screen for display. We see the television becoming a personal auto-mation, information, and communication device, fed by cable, by telephone lines, by video playback machines — even by direct satel-lite transmissions.

The telephone will also play a part in this revolution. The 1981 telephone receiver may become a collector's item, as manufacturers rush to produce phones with the latest electronic gadgets and fea-tures not available in conventional units. Home computers will be-come ubiquitous as their cost declines and software programs are created for specific repetitive tasks in the home. Financial transac-tions, shopping, education, entertainment, security services, energy management, and access to every type of data base imaginable are only a few of the things that will become available.

From the business standpoint, we see volume opportunities in ev-erything involved in the wiring of American homes with four types of personal automation hardware: cable TV, video playback devices (videocassette recorders and videodisc players), home computers, and electronic telephones.

THE EXPLOSION IN CABLE TV

In 1968 only 5 percent of the homes in the United States were wired for cable TV. By 1981 that figure had risen to 26 percent, representing 21 million homes. As shown in Exhibit 4–1, between 40 and 60 million homes could be wired for cable by the end of the decade.

The wiring of 40–60 million homes for cable represents a $10–$15 billion market. There's the basic cost of the cable itself,

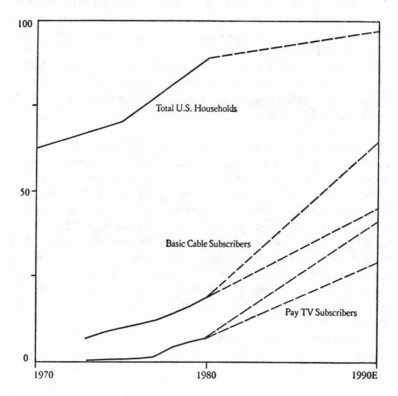

Exhibit 4 – 1
Outlook for growth in cable TV.
(Volume figures in millions of households)

($70,000 – $80,000 per mile for an underground cable), plus the cost of earth stations (which transmit and receive television signals by satellite) and head-end equipment (which processes the TV signals and transmits them through cable to subscribers).

Cable TV is booming for a number of reasons. First, the technology now exists to make cable TV a national distribution network. Back in the early-to-mid-1970s, the industry faced a major problem: how to interconnect a lot of local cable systems. Microwave transmission, the only available alternative at that time, had some serious limitations. In order to make the microwave transmission powerful enough, transmitters and receivers had to be placed every twenty miles or so, each of which needed a license from the Federal Communications Commission (FCC).

But Time Inc. and its cable subsidiary, Home Box Office (HBO), solved the problem by sending its programming via an RCA satellite to local earth stations. Many other cable operators quickly followed, and at this writing about half of all cable TV homes are getting their programming via satellite.

Other motivating forces behind the spread of cable TV are better reception of network programs, access to local programming, and a wider variety of entertainment to choose from. One of the fastest growing parts of the cable industry is pay TV, which for a monthly fee (over and above the basic monthly subscriber charge) offers a wide variety of sports events and movies. Home Box Office dominates pay cable TV, with an estimated 70 percent share of the market. Of course, as more programming becomes available, the desirability of becoming a cable subscriber will increase.

Over the long term, the greatest volume opportunities in cable TV may come from the two-way, or interactive, feature. This will allow the TV viewer to "interact" or to send a signal or communication out of the home. Two-way cable TV will also be a plus for the cable operator because it will allow fees to be generated in three ways: for the basic service, for special services, or on a per viewing basis. Also, since two-way cable will allow the cable company to document the subscriber's cable use habits, the cable company can sell this information in the same way that direct mail lists are sold.

In addition, two-way cable will have the same advantage that one-way cable has over regular over-the-air broadcasting — virtually unlimited channel offerings, each one of which could eventually appeal to a select group of viewers. Two-way cable will also make it possible to bill customers only for programs that are actually watched. From the standpoint of the supplier of quality product, this is attractive because payment is based on actual viewing hours, rather than a prenegotiated estimate. From the customer's standpoint, this arrangement is appealing because he will only pay for what he watches.

Another plus will be that the two-way cable TV operator can broadcast special-interest programming requested by a small but dedicated percentage of households. As a result of all this, two-way cable will yield substantially higher fees per household than standard cable (an estimate already borne out by a two-way cable system in Columbus, Ohio).

Finally, two-way cable will offer the potential for a range of services not now available in one place by any other means. Subscribers could get fire, burglar, and health alarms; time-shared data bases for home computers; home shopping and bill payment capabilities; home games; even market research surveys. (For instance, immediately following a presidential speech, a two-way cable audience in Columbus, Ohio, was polled concerning their reaction to the speech.)

VIDEO PLAYBACK DEVICES

In 1980 there were 2.5 million video playback devices in American homes. By 1990 we estimate the number of these devices could jump to between 50 and 75 million, as shown in Exhibit 4 – 2. That would represent volume opportunities of between $20 and $30 billion.

At this writing, there are approximately 80 million households in the United States with at least one TV set. By the end of the decade, there may be as many as 90 million such households. By 1990 we expect video playback devices to be in as many as 83 percent of TV households. In fact, RCA, a major entrant in the videodisc market, predicts that within ten years the video business will be bigger than all the TV networks combined, and double the size of the record industry.

You've probably already seen some of the advertisements for

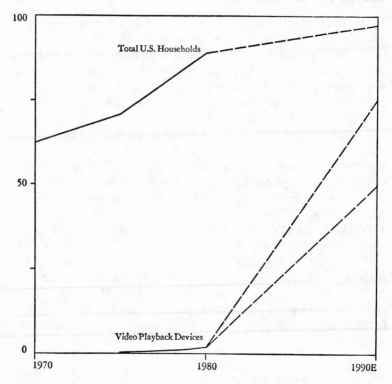

Exhibit 4 – 2
Growth potential for video playback devices.
(Volume figures in millions of households)

RCA's videodisc player and (even if you don't own a VCR), you
may have watched a videocassette recorded movie at a friend's house.
If you're like most consumers, you've probably wondered what the
relative merits of the disc versus the cassette recorder are.

Perhaps you recall how the prices of electronic calculators came
crashing down and wonder now whether the same thing will happen
to these new video products. Therefore, perhaps, you are reluctant
to spend a lot of money on cassettes or discs until you know more
about which system will be the survivor.

We focus on these questions because consumer response to the new technologies will ultimately determine how the video revolution unfolds. (The major concerns of consumers of video products and investors in the video industry are very similar.)

A videocassette recorder is an audio tape recorder with video capabilities. It is used mostly to tape sports events, old movies, or any other shows directly from the TV. A videodisc player is a machine that plays pictures on the TV set. However, a user cannot record on a videodisc; the user can only play back what has been prerecorded on it.

Although a videodisc system can theoretically do all the same things as a videocassette system, the videodiscs available to consumers over the next few years will permit only the playback of prerecorded material. Anyone who wants to record and erase or supply recorded material will have to use a videocassette machine.

Thus, until substantial quantities of prerecorded video entertainment (software) become economical, VCRs will enjoy rapid growth. Many consumers will want to use the VCR's "time-shift" capabilities, a technique by which video program material is recorded at one time and played back at another.

However, once prerecorded programs become widely accessible, videodisc players should come into their own. The reason is compelling — prerecorded videodisc material will be cheaper than blank cassettes. A videodisc requires one tenth as much surface area as a video tape to record a program. That will make the disc much cheaper than tape, which, in turn, will allow prerecorded discs, assuming they are produced in bulk, to sell for the same amount or less than a blank videocassette.

Furthermore, to duplicate a tape requires that each one be actually recorded, while discs can be duplicated by a stamping process. As you can well appreciate, it's considerably faster to stamp than to record, so the cost advantage of discs versus tape, especially in quantities of two hundred units or more, will likely continue. And the larger the production quantity of a disc, the greater the savings will be.

Is it possible that tapes could ever sell for the same price as discs? Yes. Technology is rapidly improving the efficiency with which prerecorded video tape can be duplicated; and to the extent that this happens, prerecorded tape can be priced closer to videodiscs. However, no matter how efficient the duplication process becomes, prerecorded tape will always sell at some sort of a price premium *vis-à-vis* videodiscs. Not only does tape duplication take much longer than disc stamping, but tapes are bulkier, will therefore cost more to transport and store, and will also be less attractive to space-conscious consumers.

But, you ask, what about the time-shift capability? Since videodiscs don't have it, doesn't that give a definite advantage to the cassette? Not really. When sufficient quantities of prerecorded discs become available, the consumer will have more than enough choices to pick from.

Furthermore, the time-shift feature will eventually be available on your television through the development of electronic memory circuits that are built into your TV set itself. When this happens, it will hurt the videotape market in a major way. However, built-in electronic memory circuits will probably not be available on a mass-market basis before the end of the 1980s. Thus, VCRs will continue to be an important product through 1990.

In a nutshell, we view the difference between the VCR and the videodisc player as disposable versus nondisposable, or perishable versus nonperishable. The blank cassette can be used to record literally hundreds of films or sports events that you may watch only once before you reuse the tape. But the disc, with its nondisposable nature, will become a part of your collection, as records are now.

The next critical question is, Which of the major videodisc systems will capture the bulk of the market—DiscoVision or the RCA version (SelectaVision)? We think that ultimately DiscoVision will prove the more popular because it is much more versatile.

In terms of ability to provide entertainment, the differences between the two systems are minor. But ultimately, consumer entertainment may not be the largest market. A more important source of demand may be commercial applications. For instance, if there were enough DiscoVision players in U.S. households, the telephone companies and Sears, Roebuck could put phone books and catalogs on videodiscs and distribute them to households for less than what they now spend on paper alone. Or, alternatively, educators and lecturers might use videodiscs as a major educational tool.

The advantage of DiscoVision for both the commercial and

educational markets is that it can be played forward or backward in slow or fast motion and can be stopped anywhere to a still picture (freeze-frame). Thus, a lecturer could freeze the picture to discuss a particular chart, graph, or illustration in detail. SelectaVision machines can't do this — there's no stop-action. Once the entertainment starts you have to watch it, as you would a film in a movie house.

DiscoVision has some other major advantages, too. For one thing, its information storage ability is far better than SelectaVision's. Each of the 54,000 grooves on either side of a DiscoVision disc can display a printed page, while the SelectaVision disc only has half as much storage space.

Furthermore, unlike SelectaVision, many of the DiscoVision discs have stereo sound tracks. The DiscoVision machines also have an audio jack that allows them to be plugged directly into a high-fidelity sound system, making musical performances sound much more impressive. Consumers will liken this capability to the difference between a black-and-white and a color film.

Although SelectaVision sells for less than the DiscoVision machine, a lower price won't turn out to be much of a long-term advantage. Assuming similar royalty structures and production quantities, videodiscs for both types of machines will cost the same to produce. And, as we've stressed all along, the key factor in consumer acceptance is the price of the software.

Also, the cost of producing DiscoVision may drop within the next few years. DiscoVision units currently utilize a gas laser, but by 1985 a solid-state laser may be substituted. (The disc is actually played via a beam from the laser, and thus doesn't get worn out or cracked by a stylus, which reduces wear and tear.) The gas laser is slightly bigger than a two-battery flashlight, and the solid-state laser is about the size of a thick ballpoint pen. The substitution of the solid-state laser for the gas product will probably lower DiscoVision's price to the SelectaVision level, despite DiscoVision's many incremental features.

HOME COMPUTERS

Increased penetration of video games will usher in the next round of innovations in the home — the introduction of the personal, or home, computer. You've probably seen the advertisements for Apple Computer's home computer system, and you've probably read articles about the exceptional growth potential in the market. But you're probably uncertain as to exactly what a home computer can do for you, and rightly so, because so far there isn't much of a market. Although there are computers in homes, they are generally fancy games or office-at-home machines whose uses are the same as those for a small business — financial record keeping, budgeting, and such. Another use (though presently small) is that of education. Children are learning to use computers in school and some use them at home for school problems or homework.

The lack of a market is evident when you examine the experience of small computer manufacturers. Tandy introduced its TRS-80 microcomputer in late 1977, referring to it at the time as a "home computer." Similarly, when Texas Instruments introduced the 99 / 4 in 1979, it was also billed as a "home computer."

But both companies changed their labeling rather quickly. Tandy saw that demand for its TRS-80 was exploding, with very little selling effort. The buyers, however, were small businessmen who could realize an immediate benefit.

Why should a consumer want a computer? So far, it's hard to make a good case because there are not many ways to use one. Most consumers do not find their Christmas card lists or recipe files so burdensome as to require computerization. And although financial record keeping may be a more logical application, the software must be simple and the hardware affordable and easy to understand.

A second limitation to consumer development of the home computer market is lack of knowledge of and resistance to any new product. The average consumer does not know how to program a computer and probably has no great desire to learn. And furthermore, consumers must be convinced that there is an economic benefit to owning one.

However, by the mid-1980s, both of these limitations will diminish. For one thing, literally billions of dollars will be spent by business over the next decade to bring technology to the American consumer. Whether by cable, satellite, videotape or videodisc, two-way interactive cable, or the telephone, the consumer is going to be able to receive and send a tremendous amount of information. These new communication links will provide entertainment, education, household control, and management. But all this information and data will have to be controlled. And there's only one way to do it — the home computer.

Some experts believe the United States is in transition from an industrial society to an information society. In fact, a good deal of that transition is already behind us, since 54 percent of workers in this country are currently employed in jobs that produce, process, or distribute information.

As a result of the explosion in information, it is no longer possible to be a Renaissance man with exhaustive knowledge in multiple fields. Society has grown too complex for that. The key now is knowing where to find the information on a given subject and how to gain access to it — in other words, information management.

The challenge of information management is that it has become increasingly complex. We are involved in more personal transactions and record keeping than ever before, and consequently we have greater need to call upon personalized information packages. A logical solution to the problem is some form of home computer.

Declining costs will also encourage the use of home computers. Through 1985 the memory power of semiconductors (the basis for computing power) is likely to double every two years, while the cost of producing them will keep on falling. Although these cost swings will not be fully passed on to consumers (because of increased marketing and distribution costs), low-priced personal computers may decline below their present range of $200 – $600.

The growing use of personal computers at the office will also fuel consumer demand. Many people who have used a small computer in their work now want one at home, either for their own use or for work-related applications. And many students who learn how to work with computers at school are anxious for their families to buy home computers.

Most importantly, the personal computer will eventually offer a wide range of attractive services to the consumer. In the area of communications, you could have automatic dialing of frequently called numbers as well as telephone answering. In education, you could have computer-assisted instruction. You could also have your heating, cooling, and appliances regulated by computer. In the financial area, the computer could help you with budgeting, cash-flow forecasting, and investment analysis and could arrange for the transfer of funds. You could even have your own data base, including your medical and financial records, recipes, business and personal files, calendars of activities, and lists of items to accomplish. The computer could also help out by monitoring the security of your home through fire, smoke, and burglar-detection systems.

It's important to remember that a computer is nothing more or less than memory capability. In this sense, any repetitive task in the house could eventually be tied in to computer control. Think of all the jobs around the house that could be simplified through a computer: watering the garden or lawn; paying weekly or monthly bills; turning the stove on or off; providing sufficient hot water for baths, showers, or shaving; turning up the heat in the late afternoon before you return from work; transferring important messages to friends or relatives. The list of possible benefits is only limited by your own imagination.

We think the potential for the home computer market is huge. By 1984 the market could be $1 billion, rising faster thereafter as more software comes on stream. Eventually, home computers might be found in 75–80 percent of the TV households in the United States and as many as 50 percent of the TV households in the rest of the world.

DO YOU OWN YOUR TELEPHONE?

The biggest new market of all in terms of units is the telephone. The telephone? Yes, a transformation is taking place in this business as well. The telephone that people used to rent from the phone company is on its way into oblivion. By the year 1990 Americans could own between 150 and 200 million telephones, up from less than 2 million in 1980.

This will happen because of deregulation, which allows outside suppliers to manufacture and sell telephones. Just as important is the fact that AT&T has almost completed a nationwide conversion of our telephones into a standard jack system. Thus, a new phone can be connected to the incoming telephone wire as simply and easily as putting an electrical cord into a wall socket. Once the standard jack system is completed, almost everyone will be able to buy and install a telephone produced by an independent manufacturer.

Why is the phone company installing this standard jack system? Doesn't that open the door to competition? Yes, but another problem takes precedence: the salaries of telephone repairmen have more than tripled over the past two decades. These higher labor costs could only be passed on to telephone users with difficulty and delay; thus AT&T had considerable incentive to find a way to keep installation and repair costs down, which the standard jack does, not only by eliminating the cost of installing a new telephone but also by obviating the need for repair.

The introduction of the standard jack is only one of several major changes going on in the telecommunications industry. Some experts predict that the industry will change more in the decade of the 1980s than it did in all of the previous hundred years.

The long-term impact on consumers can only be described as enormous. We will see an array of telephone and telecommunications products and services which would have seemed impossible five years ago.

Here are some of the developments that are likely to occur in the future:

- AT&T will start selling telephones.
- AT&T will probably no longer own any telephones after the late 1980s.
- AT&T will soon begin writing off the wiring inside people's homes and will stop making any further investments in wiring inside the house. Eventually, customers will own their own wiring as well as their own phones.
- AT&T will be allowed to enter markets beyond the traditional telephone industry.
- AT&T will have local "phone marts," which will become computer stores much like Tandy's Radio Shacks. In effect, they will become sales and service outlets for the telephone / computer in the home. Western Electric, AT&T's manufacturing subsidiary, will produce telephone computers and provide software and a wide range of data and memory devices.

• AT&T may adopt the latest technology much faster. It will also provide an increasing array of services, including telephone answering, message storage, and the identification of the party calling before you pick up the phone. Computer and data-processing services are not only possible, but likely.

• Telephone instruments with a wide array of convenience features will be found everywhere. We will buy phones with automatic dialing for most frequently used numbers, an automatic re-dial which will dial the number as soon as a busy line is clear, a do-not-disturb signal for owners who are having dinner or sleeping, and portable instruments that will allow you to take calls within two hundred feet of your house.

• The telephone / computer could one day be a master controller for the house, becoming, in effect, a small computer with memory. It will be capable of communicating with the outside world through the established telephone companies or through a new array of competitors. (ITT, Southern Pacific, and MCI Communications already provide competitive long-distance services to hundreds of U.S. cities. Western Union and Satellite Business Systems, an IBM-Aetna-Comsat joint venture, will soon be operating on a large scale.)

• Even the cable TV companies, with their two-way video communications capabilities, may link directly to the telephone / computer. Thus, with a phone call, you could monitor and control the temperature of your office or home and turn on or off lights, ovens, or videocassettes. The telephone / computer will also be capable of monitoring safety systems, such as smoke detectors or burglar alarms, automatically calling for emergency fire or police protection.

• Fiber optics will ultimately have the most profound impact on our telecommunications system. This technology will someday allow the telephone companies to provide multiple television channels along with the telephone signal. Eventually, a single fiber cable may carry a hundred TV channels.

Although these developments will probably seem revolutionary as they occur, a backward glance from the year 2000 will likely show how truly revolutionary were the changes in the 1980s and 90s. In the year 2000 there may be a low-cost data terminal and video display in virtually every home. Those data terminals may have large storage capacity, be controlled by an elaborate computer program, and connected to:

- one hundred or more two-way cable TV channels;
- satellite antennas providing tens or hundreds of additional channels of programming;
- the telephone companies, which will provide the equivalent of as many as a hundred lines, in addition to basic telephone service.

The amount of information capable of being received, stored, and consumed within the home in the year 2000 will be astounding.

THE COMPANIES

Tandy Corp. is the world's largest distributor of personal automation hardware. Through its Radio Shack retail outlets, Tandy has a dominant market position in consumer items and has a good position in business and professional sales.

Tandy is likely to be a major factor in the distribution of telephones, video playback units, and home computers. It has more than eight thousand stores around the world, as well as two hundred computer centers that sell and service microcomputers and related products. Thus, the distribution facilities are already in place, which is to say that the capital investment has already been made. Now it's merely a question of capitalizing on the growing consumer demand for electronics hardware.

If you haven't already been inside a Radio Shack store, you'll probably visit one within the next year or two. At some point, you may go to Radio Shack stores as frequently as once a month. Rather than being a store to visit when you need to buy a specific item, it may evolve into a store that's fun to be in, a place to drop by to find out about all the latest gadgets for the home.

Tandy's performance to date is impressive, even though the video revolution is in its earliest stages. What's more, same store sales (the real measure of growth) will benefit from new product introduction: new microcomputers, security systems, telephones, and the like. Moreover, Tandy manufactures about 49 percent of the products it sells and is increasing the self-made portion by about 2 percent annually.

While competition is increasing, Tandy's retail distribution, alert and responsive management, competitive technology, and increasing involvement in software sales could prove a potent combination.

Commodore International is a highly efficient manufacturer of personal computers. Back in the 1970s the company decided to produce its own semiconductors, which, in retrospect, was an important strategic move. This manufacturing capability has given the company the experience to innovate and experiment with new products. For instance, in 1981 it introduced the micro-mainframe, a new computer with greater versatility and power than most competing units.

Between 1978, when Commodore entered the personal computer business, and 1981, revenues from that business grew from zero to $132.4 million. In the past, Commodore focused its attention on the United Kingdom and continental Europe, but is now aggressively entering the U.S. market.

Commodore's major strategy is to capture a significant share of the home computer market (as against the business use of personal computers). Not only does this part of the market have good growth prospects, but, so far, it is less competitive.

Commodore's approach to capturing the personal computer market is threefold:

1. It manufactures as efficiently as possible in order to price the computer competitively. Commodore's in-house production of semiconductors will help accomplish this.
2. It aims for continual product innovation to capture new markets.
3. It develops extensive software capabilities for its computers. Since software is such an expensive and critical factor in consumer acceptance of computers, we think Commodore's strategy makes a lot of sense.

Scientific Atlanta could be a prime beneficiary of cable TV growth. It is a major supplier of hardware to the cable TV industry, carries a broader product line than any of its competitors, and now offers a complete line of all important products used in the cable industry. As we have discussed, cable TV is not entirely a network of underground cable lines. The actual programming is frequently transmitted via satellite to the region where the cable system is located. Scientific Atlanta has an important position in this business, with a high percentage of the market for earth stations (which transmit and receive television signals by satellite) and head-end equipment (which processes the TV signals and transmits them through cable to subscribers).

The company's strong market position is corroborated by a remarkable corporate performance. For the ten-year period ending June 30, 1981, Scientific Atlanta had not reported one declining quarter in either revenues or earnings.

The growth prospects for earth stations and satellite communications products continue to look favorable. Eventually earth stations may be located at almost every cable TV or broadcast facility. Earth stations may deliver TV programs to hotels, apartment complexes, and many individual homes.

Besides cable TV, Scientific Atlanta has good prospects in set-top converters and business satellite communications systems. The company currently produces a fifty-four channel set-top converter, which is aiming at a potential five-year market of $500-750 million. Scientific Atlanta is particularly optimistic about business applications for earth stations, with delivery of programs to offices, factories, and ships. The company sees the business market as a larger one than cable TV by the latter half of the decade.

Many households cannot be wired for cable economically. Either the terrain is too hostile or the population is too spread out. By 1990 there will be apparently 20 million households that fall into this category.

We believe that at least 3 million of these households will eventually get their TV programs through direct broadcast satellite systems operated by *Communications Satellite Corp.* (COMSAT). And that figure may prove conservative because there are 4.6 million households today that receive only one or two TV broadcast channels. COMSAT's service will likely provide three channels of subscription television service: a subscription service like HBO, a children's / special events channel, and an educational / sports channel. With the basic service to be priced around $16 a month and the antenna and electronic equipment renting for $8 a month, the monthly subscriber cost appears to be low enough to achieve good market penetration of those homes not passed by cable.

COMSAT will also benefit from growth in business satellite communications through its joint venture with IBM and Aetna. This venture provides private line satellite services to large business customers.

Unfortunately, there is no pure way of participating in the manufacturing end of video playback devices. The Japanese dominate the manufacturing part of this business, and the only way to participate directly in the production side is through the large Japanese trading or electronics companies.

CHAPTER 5

Video Entertainment

Star Wars, Raiders of the Lost Ark, Superman, Jaws, Gone With the Wind . . . you've probably seen at least one of these films, perhaps even all — but we'll venture a guess that almost no one saw these movies for the first time on their TV screen.

Ever since the inception of the film industry, most new-release movie watching has taken place in theaters. This may change in the years ahead, and not necessarily at the expense of the movie house.

The video revolution will make it possible for you to watch what you want when you want where you want. Once the new technology is in place in the home, consumers will have a huge selection of new entertainment to choose from. You'll be able to watch the latest movies right in the comfort of your own living room — whenever it's most convenient for you.

How many times has a movie at your local theater moved away before you've had a chance to see it? Are you often late to movies because you can't quite make it in time for, say, the 7:45 P.M. showing? Or do you avoid going to movies altogether because you dislike standing in line or watching a film in a crowded, noisy movie theater? If so, you are likely to be an avid user of the new technologies and an enthusiastic participant in the video revolution.

The beauty of the software, or entertainment, side of this business is its repeat nature. Once the hardware is in the home, business opportunities in that area are largely restricted to product innovation and replacement. But software has no such limitations.

The relationship between hardware and software is somewhat analogous to that between razors and razor blades. You'll purchase a new razor once every several years, but you need new razor blades every week. Thus blades, not razors, are the real bread-and-butter part of the business. Likewise, we think the real opportunities in the consumer electronics business lie in the unlimited potential for software development and sales.

Table 6 presents our view of the growth potential of the consumer video software market in the United States. We see total U.S. personal consumption expenditures increasing from $1,670 billion in 1980 to $4,745 billion in 1990. But more importantly, the percentage of spending on consumer information / communications might increase from 2.9 percent of the total in 1980 to as much as 4 percent by 1990, with the video-related share of that figure jumping dramatically from 5.2 percent of the total to 20 – 40 percent. On this basis, we estimate that the total amount of spending on consumer video software in 1990 in the United States might be $35 – 75 billion annually, as large a yearly market as we estimate for hardware for the entire decade.

Table 6

U.S. VIDEO-RELATED CONSUMER SOFTWARE MARKET

	1980 ($ billions)	1990E ($ billions)	% compound annual growth rate
Total personal consumption expenditures (PCE)	1,670	4,745	11
Consumer information / communications expenditures	48	189	15
% PCE	2.9	4.0	
Video-related information / communications expenditures	2.5	35 – 75	30 – 40
% of total consumer information / communica- tions expenditures	5.2	20 – 40	

WHAT WILL THE VIDEO-RELATED SOFTWARE CONSIST OF?

What sort of video information or entertainment will be available in 1990? The answer to this question, as we've implied all along, is of interest not only to investors, but also to entrepreneurs. Very little of the software presently exists, which means someone is going to have to create it. The multibillion dollar market we are suggesting for 1990 will encourage the start-up of literally hundreds of new businesses.

We believe the coming software revolution will involve five basic elements: information, entertainment, education, transactions (paying bills, transferring funds, and the like) and shopping. Information and entertainment will clearly be the two largest markets over the near term, with the other three showing longer-term potential. We discussed some aspects of software in the last chapter, but other possibilities exist, too:

- twenty-four-hour-a-day news
- electronically transmitted newspapers
- college courses for credit
- adult entertainment
- video shopping, which uses a TV screen to feature such products as washers, books, or even entire catalogs of merchandise
- access to data banks, which can provide any specific piece of information needed, for instance travel information, or background on a particular subject, country, individual, or company
- stock and financial market services and information

By the same token, consumer shopping sophistication will increase significantly in the next few years. The average retail customer will feel relatively comfortable using electronic equipment both for purchasing and for pleasure. Phone purchasing will certainly be a reality. Customers at home will be able to call central service areas (retail stores or distribution centers) and buy many basic items. Consumers will probably have an identification number which will be acceptable for all purchases. As a result of these advances, phone purchasing could account for more than 15 percent of general merchandise sales by the 1990s.

We also think some form of a charge card could be available by 1990, which customers might use for anything from groceries to leisure activities. In order to facilitate consumer spending, banks might develop a sophisticated money transfer system.

More significantly, people may be able to carry on a multitude of business and communication activities between their homes and offices or other homes via equipment tied into the electronic network. Of course, we will all have to become better trained in the use of home computers and other equipment in order to take full advantage of all the available data.

By the year 2000, master computers may be keyed into every sort of activity you can imagine. We may be able to plan vacations completely from our own homes without outside assistance, including making and confirming reservations, calculating the cost of the trip to the last dollar, and planning a full itinerary. Indeed, this is only the tip of the iceberg, and we will probably have a variety of fuel-efficient and productive household items and resources that would boggle the mind today.

Demand for software will come from three major businesses: cable TV operators who need to fill an expanding number of channels; the owners of video playback devices who will want more and more entertainment; and users of personal computers who will need extensive programming.

Finding a pure, riskless way to participate in the software side of the video revolution is not easy because events are unfolding quickly and congressional legislation could affect the outcome dramatically. Nevertheless, we have identified several broad investment areas that could benefit from the software explosion: companies that own large libraries of video software (the major film companies); companies that make the software (again the major film companies); companies that serve the film production industry, technically or artistically; companies that are investing heavily in electronic-based education systems; and certain newspaper companies that have expanded into cable TV and electronic publishing and are now aggressively developing their own programming.

THE FILM INDUSTRY WILL BENEFIT

Although it's still too early to predict the size and makeup of the coming video market, it is clear that film-making skill and libraries of film software are both assets with increasing value. With the emergence of two new industries that consume filmed entertainment product — cable TV and video playback devices — we are already seeing good growth in the use of filmed entertainment.

As recently as 1977, not even the most optimistic expert claimed that these three areas together purchased $100 million of filmed entertainment product annually. Yet in 1981 we estimate that cable TV alone purchased over $400 million worth of theatrical films. Furthermore, we calculate that the wholesale value of prerecorded videocassette sales exceeded $100 million in 1981. While videodisc sales are not yet significant, they will be a growing force. As we discussed earlier, the videodisc hardware cannot record and thus will depend largely on theatrical films for its software.

Traditionally, the major outlet for films has been the motion picture theater. In recent years the film industry has collected rentals from the domestic theater industry of $1 – 1.25 billion a year, as well as another $750 million annually in rentals to foreign markets. The other purchaser of film is the domestic television industry, which has spent about $500 million annually in recent years. Thus, at this writing, the annual wholesale market for the U.S. film industry can be estimated as follows:

Table 7

ESTIMATED ANNUAL U.S. FILM INDUSTRY REVENUES

Source	($ billions)
U.S. theaters	1. – 1.25
Foreign theaters	0.75
U.S. television	0.50
Videocassettes	0.10
Cable TV	0.40
Miscellaneous	0.20
	2.95 – 3.20

Although some think that the amount of money paid by the network TV broadcasting companies to the film industry will drop as the income from the pay cable TV companies rises, we do not agree. It is our view that pay cable TV companies and TV broadcasters will bid against each other for theatrical products to the benefit of the film companies and to the detriment of the network TV broadcasting and pay cable TV companies.

In our opinion, theatrical films that are properly merchandised and scheduled represent the strongest competitive weapon for both the network TV broadcasting and the cable TV companies in the battle to achieve audience market share leadership.

Table 8 shows the current situations and our forecasts for the future for network and cable TV. As you can see, we expect pay cable TV and its spending on theatrical films to grow rapidly.

Table 8

THEATRICAL FILM EXPENDITURES
(in thousands)

	No. of TV households	Broadcasting expenditures on theatrical films	No. of pay cable TV households	Pay cable TV expenditures on theatrical films	Total expenditures on theatrical films
1985E	87,000	$790,000	35,000	$1,100,000	$1,890,000
1981	80,000	550,000	14,500	400,000	950,000
1975	69,600	400,000	18	500	400,500

So far, the new technologies (videocassettes and videodiscs) are not spending anywhere near as much money on films as regular TV and cable TV are, but that gap should narrow in the years ahead, as the next table suggests.

Table 9

PRERECORDED VIDEO PRODUCT SALES[a]
(in thousands)

	Videocassette recorder sales (units)	Prerecorded videocassettes (wholesale)	Videodisc players (units)	Videodisc sales (wholesale)	Total sales prerecorded video products (wholesale)
1990E	4,500	$1,000,000	5,000	$650,000	$1,650,000
1985E	3,500	440,000	2,000	150,000	590,000
1980	780	85,000	40	2,500	87,500
1979	470	40,000	4	200	40,200
1978	400	20,000			2,000

[a] Prerecorded videocassette estimates are based on the assumption that unit sales will approximate three units for each VCR in the first year after sale and one unit for each VCR after the first year. Wholesale prices are assumed to be $20 – 30 per unit. Videodisc estimates are based on the assumption that unit sales will approximate five units for each player in the first year after sale and three units for each player after the first year. Wholesale disc prices are assumed to be $7.00 – 8.00.

If our forecasts in Tables 8 and 9 are accurate, film companies will clearly experience rapid growth in sales of their products and services over the next five years. By 1990 wholesale revenues from videocassette and videodisc sales might run as high as $1,650 million a year — up from only $100 million in 1981.

Note that all of our projections are adjusted for two problems that tarnish slightly the bright outlook: rentals and pirating. It has been found that most people prefer renting videocassettes to buying them outright, but until recently, almost every film company was trying to discourage these rentals and promote outright sales. This resulted in the formation of many successful rental operations, a challenge to which we believe the film industry will eventually respond by developing an effective rental program, thereby generating revenues even beyond those we project here.

Pirating (or home taping of films) is a problem that has troubled the film industry for many years, and with the development of videotape the problem has gotten worse. No matter what, it will remain a drain on potential sales through the end of the decade. However, things may improve with the growing popularity of videodiscs — because the discs will be priced below the price of blank tape, and it will therefore be cheaper to buy a disc than to tape a cassette.

Large-scale commercial pirating may also be reduced by the advent of videodiscs. Today, anyone with a videocassette recorder can get into the commercial pirating business because it is difficult to track down the producers of the pirated product. But videodiscs, while very cheap on a per-unit basis, require expensive capital equipment for reproduction. Thus, videodisc pirates will be much more visible and much easier to apprehend.

THE COMPANIES

All of the above factors combine to make a good case for looking closely at the companies associated with the creation and ownership of films, and certain media companies.

Unfortunately, there are only five public film companies to choose from: Warner Communications Inc., Reeves Communications, MCA Inc., Walt Disney Productions, and Metro-Goldwyn-Mayer Film Co. Note that other companies, such as Compact Video, Gulf & Western Industries, Metromedia, Taft Broadcasting, Telecommunications

Industries, Time Inc., Viacom, and Video Corporation of America are not extensively in the business of creating film, don't own significant film assets, or are in this business in a relatively small way compared with their other operations.

Warner Communications is involved in all aspects of the software business: film creation, software for cable TV, software for personal computers, and software for video playback devices. Historically, Warner's two leading businesses have been recorded music and motion pictures. But it is fast becoming a major force in all of the important new technologies we have discussed in this chapter.

Even at this early stage in their development, pay cable TV, videocassettes, videodiscs, and satellite TV transmission are earning Warner's film division millions of dollars a year in additional revenues. So far, Atari, Warner's toy and game division, is emerging as the company's single largest earnings source, primarily from home video and coin-operated games. Warner also owns 50 percent of Warner-Amex Cable, which (depending on what statistics you use) represents the fifth or the third largest cable TV system in the United States. Furthermore, its cable operation is one of the fastest-growing systems in the country, having won approximately 60 percent of all the cable TV franchises awarded in 1980. Warner's two-way cable system, called QUBE, is still the only way to capitalize on the long-term prospects for two-way cable. Through its Warner Brothers theatrical film business, the company is a major producer of films and owns an extensive film library that is becoming increasingly valuable. Last but not least, the Warner-Amex Satellite Entertainment Co. has become one of the top two suppliers of specialized programming to the nation's rapidly growing cable TV network.

Warner's management believes the personal computer will eventually have greater sales potential than its video computer system, which is where the two-way cable capability will come in handy. A computer on the consumer end of a two-way cable system could store vast amounts of material and information, thereby freeing up the same channel for other uses.

Within three to five years the Warner-Amex cable TV system will probably be serving 3 million homes. While it does not seem feasible to get a majority of these households to buy a personal computer, it is possible that most households would rent a computer for $20, $30, or $40 per month, in much the same way that a cable subscriber pays for service.

Reeves Communications is a medium-sized company that is gearing up to capitalize on the growth of video products. The company was originally in the business of acquiring TV programs for select corporate clients, but has since moved into the production of TV programs, made-for-TV movies, and theatrical films. The company is also involved in direct-to-the-home merchandising, primarily of books, and the rental of TV production facilities to others.

Reeves' management is keenly aware of the coming video revolution and has the staff to create, refine, and distribute new products. Reeves will likely be at the forefront of new product development, as the new technologies start to generate more revenues for films than network TV.

MCA Inc. is another film company that could benefit from the video revolution. For one thing, sales of film products are becoming increasingly important to the company. Even more important, MCA is the world's leading producer and owner of software, which puts it in a strong position as video's appetite for new material grows.

Time Inc. started the video revolution back in 1975 when it introduced national pay cable TV services. With over 70 percent of the pay cable TV market and over 4 million subscribers, Time is both the largest cable TV operator by far and the largest factor in software delivery for the cable TV market.

Time is also the largest book and magazine publisher in the United States, businesses that will benefit indirectly from the video revolution. Moreover, it is engaged in a number of related graphic arts and training information fields and is a significant producer of building materials, pulp, paperboard, containerboard, and containers.

Certain newspaper chains are also well positioned. Many of them are purchasing cable TV systems and developing their own programming. Because of their experience in providing information and entertainment to the consumer and the home, they are likely to be able to capitalize on the technologies. While it may seem farfetched to think of reading your morning newspaper on a video screen, the reality is quickly approaching.

Times Mirror Co. is the most widely and significantly diversified information company in the United States. The core of the company is its newspaper group, particularly the Los Angeles *Times,* which carries more advertising lineage than any other newspaper in the world. In 1980 Times Mirror added the five television stations owned by the Newhouse Newspapers group to its Broadcast and Cable Television Group, making Times Mirror an important power in broadcasting as well as newspapers.

So far, Times Mirror's activities in the electronic area are modest, but they're growing fast. At the end of 1980 the company had 571,000 cable subscribers, of whom 300,000 had signed up for Spotlight, its pay cable TV answer to Home Box Office.

Times Mirror is also experimenting with Telidon, a Canadian videotext service. ("Videotext" is the generic expression for the wired home of the future.) This service is an interactive, information-on-demand service that can use either cable TV or telephone. Times Mirror also offers Shopping Channel to its cable TV subscribers in a video shopping experiment.

In addition, Times Mirror is a major publisher of books and magazines, and, like Time, is engaged in a number of related fields. Furthermore, it is also vertically integrated into newsprint and forest products materials.

Multimedia Inc. is the only publicly held small-city newspaper chain centered in the rapidly growing southeast United States. Increasingly oriented toward electronic media, in 1980 Multimedia derived nearly two thirds of its operating profits from radio broadcasting and cable TV operations. It owns six TV and twelve radio stations, as well as Multimedia Productions, Inc., the producers of such shows as "The Phil Donahue Show," "The Bob Braun Show," and Young People's and Country Music Specials.

At this writing, the company's cable TV operations, which have about 70,000 subscribers, with the potential of some 200,000 by 1984, comprise one of the most ambitious cable development projects by a company of its size. Multimedia's programming has also been innovative and in 1980 accounted for 12 percent of its revenues, one of the highest percentages in the industry. Its newspapers and broadcasting operations are doing better than the industry average, which reflects not only the above-average economic environment in its region, but also top-quality management.

Harte-Hanks Communications is built upon a chain of small-city newspapers based in the rapidly growing Southwest, particularly Texas. On that foundation, it has established a significant broadcasting and cable TV business and has created a unique consumer distribution marketing operation to capitalize on the growing fragmentation of the consumer sector and on the need for advertisers to reach a specific audience. In the 1980s the company plans to focus on four growth areas: cable TV, consumer marketing, entertainment software, and electronic information services.

In our opinion, Harte-Hanks, which owns eight cable TV operations and manages another seventeen, has long held one of the clearest visions and most effective strategies for this new age of information and has maintained one of the best earnings growth rates in the industry.

Harte-Hanks is presently experimenting in electronic publishing with CompuServe and the Associated Press. A simple phone call to a central computer system will give consumers with home computers electronic access to the articles in that day's newspaper.

One final company should probably be discussed in this chapter. Although the new video technologies will lead to a greater number of people watching filmed entertainment than ever before, we are not going to become mere vegetables in front of a TV screen. In fact, as you can gather from our comments about the videodisc in the last chapter, we think education may eventually become a major market.

Those who are familiar with the U.S. public and private school systems know that the computer is already part of modern education. Computers have been found to be good teaching and research aids, and a whole generation of young people are growing up familiar with the computer.

The major way to participate in the growing use of the new technologies in education is through *SFN Companies, Inc.* (formerly Scott, Foresman & Company), a large book publishing operation. SFN could revolutionize the method of teaching in this country; already it has persuaded many school systems throughout the country that children can learn better with computers. SFN's work in the area, we believe, could well make it the major supplier of educational software to our schools.

CHAPTER 6

Office Automation Hardware

The same technological revolution going on in the home is also changing the face of the world of business. Within the next decade, most of the clerical functions of commerce will be affected by computers and memory power.

One of the first harbingers of the future was the automation of airline ticket reservations. Now, all the airline counter clerk need do is punch a few letters and numbers into a local computer terminal to confirm your reservation. The same efficiency is also available at large hotels, particularly nationwide hotel chains. When you call for a reservation on a particular date, the clerk can immediately tell you if any rooms are available and equally quickly record your reservation on the central computer.

What makes this possible is the increasing use of what's called "distributed data processing" (i.e., local distribution and accumulation of data as opposed to the centralized system that used to be so prevalent).

In the late 1960s, for instance, many large corporations acquired huge computers for their headquarters. The problem with this was that the employees out in the field or at local branch offices had no data-processing capabilities.

Imagine if hundreds of local offices had to phone in to one central office. Not only would the telephone lines be constantly jammed, but customers would have to wait in line endlessly, and no doubt the information given them would not be up to date, anyway.

Distributed data processing solves these problems by providing "intelligent" terminals out in the field. Not only can these local terminals record information, but they have access to the files in the central computer. Thus, when the clerk at the airline counter confirms your ticket reservation, he or she is doing so through the use of distributed data processing.

The computerization of airline and hotel reservations is just the beginning of widespread automation of individual business tasks. In effect, we are going to put the computer at the service of the individual office worker. It is hoped that by doing so we can reverse our declining productivity, a subject of growing national concern. Two of our most widely read and prestigious business publications have highlighted the plight of our declining industrial base, and most Americans are now aware of our lagging productivity, especially in comparison with the Japanese.

Almost every economist agrees that the best way to raise productivity is capital investment that will improve efficiency, reduce costs, or increase output per worker. But business won't invest the money unless there is a clear economic reason for doing so. Well, the rapidly falling price of computer technology has created a forceful economic rationale since the payback on a new-technology investment is often two years or less. What's more, as the cost of technology hardware declines further, the economics will become even more attractive. By 1985 the $3,000 computer for individual use will have two to three times the capability of today's $3,000 unit.

Exhibit 6–1 illustrates how rising labor costs and declining costs of computer technology have brought about a dramatic shift in relative price. A 1981 $18,000 small business computer system would have cost over $100,000 in 1970 — representing a drop in price of 16 percent a year. Meanwhile, the cost of using labor instead of computer power rose 7 percent a year during the same period. Through 1985 the cost of technology will certainly continue to drop as labor costs increase, thereby accelerating the relative price advantage of computers. And looking farther ahead, there appear to be no technological barriers to prevent this trend from continuing beyond the end of this century. (However, average unit prices aren't expected to decline much. Rather, the bulk of the price improvement will come from vastly improved capability per unit.)

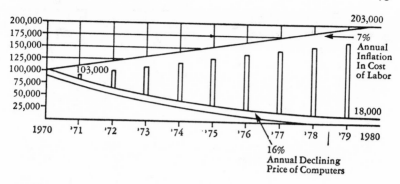

Exhibit 6 – 1
The relative price of labor versus computing power.

Another force behind office automation is the greater understanding by the user of how to employ computers. The traditional large data processing system was rigid, complex, and very intimidating for many users. But, personal automation devices are different in that they are small, self-contained, powerful, and flexible devices entirely under the user's control. What's more, a rapidly growing number of entrepreneurs are developing the easy-to-use software packages required to make personal computing devices workable for the uninitiated.

Unfortunately, quantifying the market for the office of the future resists simple analysis. The distinction between the products that will help in office automation (e.g., computers, telephones, and other telecommunications equipment) is blurry, to say the least. And yet, traditional analysis that bundles many products together into the computer / office products category misses the exceptional growth opportunities in this industry.

The magnitude of the growth potential can be seen in looking at just one part of the market — what we call "personal automation devices" — in effect, small business computers, intelligent terminals, and word processing systems. As shown in Exhibit 6 – 2, 1980 shipments of these products amounted to approximately $2.5 billion. Assuming a growth rate of 30 – 40 percent per year over the decade,

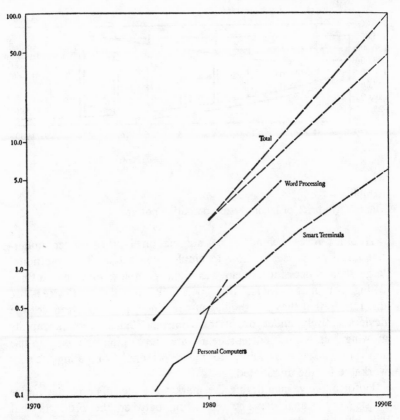

Exhibit 6–2
Growth potential for personal automation devices.

which appears reasonable judging by current trends, we could have
a market in 1990 of $25 – 50 billion a year.

Many studies have attempted to quantify the potential market for
automated office products. The gloomy economic outlook may affect
the market for the time being. But eventually, as the recession ends
and corporate profits increase from their dismal 1982 level, the demand for office automation should expand. The basic reasons for this
are as follows:

● The service sector of the economy is growing much more rapidly than the farm or manufacturing sectors, and by 1990 an es-

timated 90 million people will be employed in white collar positions in the United States.

- With the number of people entering the work force declining, it is imperative that business improve productivity in order to grow and maintain profitability. Since farming and manufacturing are nearly fully automated, this suggests productivity improvements will have to come from office automation.

- The capital investment per farm worker in the United States averages over $50,000, and the capital investment per factory worker averages over $30,000. Yet the capital investment per office worker averages only $2,500. Thus, if the average capital investment per office worker were to rise to only 20 percent of that of the factory worker by 1990, we would have a new market of over $300 billion.

Note that the computer revolution of the 1980s will be vastly different from that of the 1950s and 1960s. That's because today's real need for computing power is at the individual level. But such needs cannot be served or satisfied by a mass-marketing approach. The real growth potential, as we see it, lies not in the big computer companies, but rather in the small, entrepreneurial, problem-solving businesses that are rapidly building market bases.

We believe there are three areas in office automation that should show growth for most of the 1980s: word processing, financial transactions, and telecommunications equipment. Let's now look briefly at each one and discuss some of the companies that appear to be well positioned.

WORD PROCESSING: ITS TIME HAS COME

Word processing can do wonders for secretarial efficiency. Let's say you are a lawyer working on a ten-page contract between two corporations. The contract must go through numerous drafts, as lawyers from both corporations add, insert, or delete paragraphs, sentences, or words. A word processor allows a typist to store the first draft electronically and thereafter to make any specific line changes that are necessary. Then, when the draft reflects the modifications, the typist instructs the word processor to type out the contract on paper. The amount of secretarial typing time that can be saved with such equipment is obviously considerable.

Word processors can be used for business letters, book manuscripts, internal memorandums — indeed, for any piece of writing which will have more than one draft. Word processors are also particularly useful for producing a large quantity of identical letters. Let's say you are a stock broker with five hundred regular customers. To type individual letters to each would be very time-consuming, but with a word processor, once you have composed your letter, the machine does all the work of typing and even addressing the many copies, freeing your secretary for other tasks.

While estimates of the market size for word processors vary widely, from a base of 35,000 keyboards in 1977, we estimate the total population could eventually grow to some 20 million keyboards by 1990.

We believe that the distinction between stand-alone and clustered keyboards is blurring as manufacturers develop systems which can be hooked together at reasonable cost. Thus, the argument that clustered systems will prove more popular because of the lower price per keyboard has weakened considerably.

For this reason, we regard the market for word processing equipment as a homogeneous one, with estimated 1980 shipments in the United States of around 110,000 keyboards, or $1.4 billion (including software), and 130,000 keyboards worldwide, or $1.7 billion. By the mid-1980s we expect this market to grow to about 400,000 keyboards in the United States, or $5 billion (including software), and 520,000 keyboards worldwide, or $6.5 billion.

Who is going to benefit from this growing market? We think *NBI Inc.* appears to be well positioned. NBI designs, develops, manufactures, services, and markets software-based word processing systems. In all of the company's products, an operator types on an electronic keyboard and the text appears on a cathode-ray tube (CRT) or TV-like video display screen. The typist can make corrections or additions to the displayed text before it is printed. The system stores the typed information on fixed disks or removable magnetic diskettes for future use.

NBI's first products, System I and System II, gave way in May 1978 to its principal current product, System 3000, a stand-alone display word processor with an optional extra work station (screen plus keyboard), extra disk storage, enhanced software capabilities, and several alternative printers.

NBI has put together a unique management team and outstanding products that have won it a 2 percent share of worldwide shipments in 1979 and 4 percent in 1980, which may rise to perhaps as much as 6 percent by the mid-1980s.

In an environment where products become obsolete every two years and the competition is led by the likes of IBM, Xerox, and Digital Equipment, the primary assets to look for in a potential investment are quality of product, quality of support, manufacturing expertise, quality of personnel, and financial stability. NBI appears strong in these areas:

● *Quality of product:* NBI's equipment typically rates with the top companies in terms of options, flexibility, ease of use, reliability, and cost / performance.

● *Quality of support:* NBI's sales force is held in generally high regard; in terms of service, training, and support, it gets high marks.

● *Manufacturing expertise:* NBI has good operations managers, with extensive background in the data processing industry.

● *Quality of personnel:* NBI has put together a management team capable of steering the company to a multi-hundred-million-dollar size without significant disruptions. It has attracted first-rate people from Xerox, Data General, and Storage Technology and is in fact turning away highly qualified salesmen because it doesn't want to grow too fast. The company also has one of the lowest employee turnover rates in the industry.

● *Financial Stability:* So far, NBI has had a return on investment of 24 percent and a return on shareholders' equity of 24 percent.

THE AUTOMATION OF FINANCIAL TRANSACTIONS: NO MORE WAITING IN BANK LINES

No matter where you live, you've probably had to spend many unnecessary hours waiting in line at the bank. No matter how many tellers a bank has, there always seem to be too many customers. Well, the same individualized automation that has revolutionized airline and hotel reservations and is boosting the productivity of secretaries is also affecting the transfer of funds and the deposit or withdrawal of money and cash.

Bank lines are being shortened in many locations through automated teller machines (ATMs) and cash dispensers. Some of these facilities speed service and relieve congestion inside the bank. Others are located outdoors to permit twenty-four-hour access or in supermarkets and other retail stores. Finally, some are being placed at remote locations where there's no branch office nearby, effectively creating a new, limited-facility branch.

Part of the increase of ATMs stems from the growing demand for bank lobby machines—not to assist human tellers, but actually to replace them. This is occurring for two reasons. First, these ATMs are much less expensive than their outdoor counterparts, which require additional security and have higher operational costs. Second, as labor costs rise, replacing human tellers with electronic ones becomes increasingly attractive.

Ultimately, the real growth area in financial transactions is electronic funds transfer (EFT), which can be simply defined as the increased use of computers to transfer money in and out of your bank account for the payment of bills. Although there are still substantial regulatory obstacles and stiff consumer resistance to EFT, it will probably eventually succeed since it saves us time, provides us with twenty-four-hour access to our money, protects us from theft and unauthorized use of checks, and will reduce a bank's processing costs because electronic payment transactions are inherently more efficient than existing paper-based methods. EFT is slowly emerging from red tape and regulation and now seems well on its way to becoming a multibillion-dollar market for data processing manufacturers by 1990.

But the ultimate implications of EFT for consumers and those who will take advantage of its services (primarily retailers and banks) are much greater. "Electronic funds transfer" is really a catch-all term that can be applied to any number of systems that do not presently interact. However, at some point, all transactions processed by electronic means will become part of a vast national network. In a completely electronic system, a money transaction for a purchase could be made at any machine, with the purchaser's bank account immediately charged and the vendor's account immediately credited.

This unified national computer network is far in the future because of regulatory problems at the state and local level, as well as resistance from consumers who see it as a threat to their control over personal finances and as an invasion of privacy. With time, however, this national network will probably be implemented since there are some very real benefits to be derived for all concerned. Consumers could get sizable reductions in the direct expenses involved in paying bills. For instance, checking account charges and postage costs would be largely eliminated and the consumer could save considerable time by having bills paid automatically. The payee receives the benefits of immediate use of funds and bad checks become impossible.

The several different methods of making electronic bill payments all eliminate written checks — a direct benefit to the financial institutions that would otherwise have to process them. Telephone bill-paying systems appear to be the most likely way to go — and over two hundred independent systems are already in existence in the United States. There are several variations on the telephone payment systems, but they all offer bank customers the ability to designate bills to be paid to specific creditors, in specific amounts and on selected dates. The financial institution makes an appropriate debit to the customer's designated account and forwards the payment electronically to the proper recipient.

One thing is certain: widespread EFT would have a dramatic impact on the manufacturers of the new technology, on consumers, on retailers, and on financial institutions. The manufacturers of EFT equipment should have a substantial market, exceeding $1 billion by 1990 for terminal equipment alone and three times that size if data processing hardware, software, and services were included.

For the consumer, the future holds reduced time needed for and cost of paying bills, increased returns on savings (as payments can be made directly from interest-bearing accounts), but loss of float on both checks and credit cards. Eventually shop-at-home terminals will be available to direct the appropriate transfer of funds.

For the retailer, EFT will allow increased customer traffic, reduced labor expenses, reduction of losses in check cashing and charge-card payments, and expanded markets through shop-at-home services.

For financial institutions, we foresee reduced operational expenses and increased competition among financial services companies to provide total service.

Until EFT comes into its own, the best way to participate in what's happening is through the largest and most rapidly growing submarket of EFT, the ATM and its more modest counterpart, the cash dispenser.

One company well situated to benefit from the particular growth in ATMs, as well as from the general emergence of EFT, is *ISC Systems Corp.*, which designs, manufactures, sells, and services on-line teller terminal systems that assist financial institutions in rapid, efficient processing of customer transactions.

ISC could benefit from a number of important trends:

• The market ISC serves is large and still growing. The U.S. replacement market for automated teller terminals in the savings and loan (S&L) industry, where ISC is well entrenched, is currently about $600 million in annual revenues. But since the market is less than 25 percent saturated, we don't expect it to become mature until 1985, at the earliest. The total U.S. market for these teller terminals is about $1.7 billion, and the total worldwide market is estimated to be $3.3 billion.

• Bank deregulation, competitive pressures, and the cost of labor are forcing U.S. financial institutions to automate their teller functions.

• With a unique knowledge of the U.S. S&L industry, ISC has been able to put together a product combining hardware and software that presently appears to have a clear technological edge over the competition. This has allowed the company to gain a 29 percent share of the installed base of modular terminals and a 30 percent (but rising) share of shipments.

• ISC should be able to develop a product for the commercial bank and international market — which could mean 6 – 8 years of solid growth potential.

In any company that is experiencing such fast growth, there are risks. We would keep close track of the following:

    • ISC's immediate expertise lies in a highly specialized market segment without unlimited growth potential. By 1983 the company must successfully diversify into commercial banking and by 1986–87 into the international markets.

- The pressures on U.S. financial institutions may prove so severe that they automate faster than forecast and faster than ISC can capitalize on with its small revenue base. This would result in market saturation sooner than anticipated, a potential limit to growth.
- Management appears top-heavy with experience in the thrift industry. It would be reassuring to see talent drawn from commercial banking.
- Managing the type of growth that ISC has had is very difficult.

THE AUTOMATION OF TELECOMMUNICATIONS

Business telephone efficiency is also being vastly improved by computer technology. Perhaps you've encountered some of these new developments yourself; you might, for instance, have recently called a business acquaintance only to learn that he or she has a new direct dial number, thus bypassing any backlog at a central switchboard. This is possible through what's called a PBX (private branch exchange) system — which can best be described as telephone switches at the users' location that automatically direct incoming or internal phone calls.

The advantage of the PBX system can be appreciated by those who remember what it was like in the late 1960s when most business phone systems were incapable of handling any dramatic increase in phone calls. Many brokerage houses were so inundated with calls during the stock market boom of the late 1960s that customers were frequently unable to get through for hours at a time.

Deregulation too, as we saw in Chapter 4, is affecting the market for telecommunications equipment. In fact, the independent suppliers of telecommunications equipment to business are an outgrowth of the FCC's Carterfone decision in 1968, which gave users the right to interconnect their own communications equipment to the Bell System, so long as it did not damage facilities already in place. The decision covered all forms of terminals, including the PBX system. Through various means, AT&T was long able to stave off effective implementation of the Carterfone decision; but by 1977, interconnection was a reality and was backed by the industry, the FCC, and Congress.

Technological developments were also proceeding and advances in the price / performance relationship of computers dramatically altered the capabilities of PBX systems, thereby offering independent manufacturers an opportunity to penetrate the existing base of systems with a broad line of new products.

What are the new capabilities of the PBX system? In a nutshell, the new system uses digital switching and what's called stored program control (SPC). With earlier PBX systems it was difficult to modify features once the system was in place. But SPC permits the addition of new performance features after system installation. Most new PBX systems also use digital techniques rather than the old "analog" method to perform the switching process; the importance of this is that digital switching can handle both voice and data traffic. While such capabilities are not vital today, they'll be essential once office automation comes into its own.

Taken together, the SPC and digital switching made older PBX systems functionally obsolete and thereby opened up a whole new market to the independent companies. It's presently estimated that the 1981 installed base of PBX systems in the U.S. is between 200,000 and 215,000 units. As a result of new construction and upgrading, this installed base is probably growing at a rate of 4 – 5 percent a year. But the annual growth in revenues from new PBX systems has been running at 20 percent or more, as shown in Table 10:

Table 10

ESTIMATED U.S. SHIPMENTS OF PBX SYSTEMS
($ millions)

	1978	1979	1980	1981
PBX				
Small	$ 320	$ 385	$ 500	$ 635
Medium	760	900	1,060	1,220
Large	480	565	700	855
Total	$1,560	$1,850	$2,260	$2,710

The reason for this rapid growth rate is the rapid replacement of technologically obsolete units with newer equipment.

Will this growth rate continue in the future? We believe that it will continue once the economy recovers. However, any growth forecast is uncertain because of the difficulty of predicting replacement of existing PBX systems.

Our reasons for expecting good future growth in new PBX systems are these:

- At this writing, only 30,000 PBX systems, or less than 14 percent of total, represent state-of-the-art equipment. Thus, the replacement market will continue to thrive through the mid-1980s at least.
- The 4–5 percent unit growth rate of PBX systems could increase. Centrex units (currently estimated at 14,000–15,000) may start to be replaced by PBX systems. (Centrex is a service offered by telephone companies that provides a business with its own telephone network and some of the features of PBX systems. Usually, the Centrex switching is handled at the telephone company's central office, which is an advantage to users who want to save space. The new PBX system nullifies this advantage and should therefore penetrate the installed base of Centrex installations.)
- AT&T is raising the price on its older PBX equipment — which is pressuring its customers to upgrade to the new systems.

What of the competition? Will the small companies in this industry be squashed by large competitors? Of course, when you talk about "large competitors," you're really referring to AT&T, which had about 55 percent of the market for PBX systems in 1980. All the same, independent suppliers have captured a good portion of the market since the introduction of interconnection. The reason for this market penetration is that the independents have better technology and performance, while AT&T still does not have digital switching. (But, given its huge customer base, excellent service, marketing muscle, and the probable introduction of a digital system by 1983, AT&T must be viewed as a formidable competitor.)

The other companies in the PBX market are *General Telephone & Electronics* (9 percent), *Rolm Corp.* (11–12 percent), *Northern Telecom* (9–10 percent), and *Mitel* (7–8 percent). Companies such as *NEC, Siemens, Harris,* and *OKI* have smaller shares.

Of this group, we think *Rolm Corp*. may be well situated for the following reasons:

• Rolm's telecommunications revenues have increased nicely, as you can see:

	1976	1977	1978	1979	1980	1981
Sales ($ millions)	$9	$30	$50	$114	$201	$295

• Rolm has developed a line of compatible products. The smallest system can handle from 24 to 144 lines and the largest from 1,500 to 4,000 lines. Each different system can combine with every other, and the user can switch from one product to the next with no problems as more lines are needed. This capability is unique to Rolm.

• By 1984 Rolm should have a direct sales force in all the major markets in the United States. Among the other independent vendors today, only Northern Telecom and Harris are capable of such a marketing effort.

• Rolm is the most successful independent in the PBX industry, having gained the number one position by 1979 from a zero base. The reasons behind this success are:

- A background as a computer company, which enabled Rolm's management to see that digital computer concepts, not telecommunications techniques, would dominate PBX system design. Rolm has continued to stay ahead of the competition from a technological standpoint.
- Heavy emphasis on product quality and responsive marketing research.
- The best conceived, executed, and supported marketing strategy of the independents.

CHAPTER 7

Information Vending

How our attitude toward business news has changed! Once confined to the back pages of newspapers and magazines, business and financial news now often dominates the front pages. One of the most prominent examples of the growing importance of keeping abreast of events in the world of business and finance is the phenomenal growth in circulation of *The Wall Street Journal*.

It should come as no surprise that business information is in great demand. For one thing, the world of business has rarely been in a period of greater flux. The U.S. economy is no longer closed, and economic and political events in other parts of the world have a dramatic effect on the business outlook. New technological developments, rapid changes in relative prices, and deregulation are also roiling the economic picture. Finally, today's political and economic instability and the public's lack of confidence in the future have created greater volatility than at any time since the 1930s. All this contributes to the public's need to know.

We believe that business information requirements, like other matters we have discussed, are likely to be individualized and personal in nature. And thus, the only limits on the demand for business information are our imaginations.

A marketing specialist at General Foods might want immediate access to a ten-year comparison of U.S. economic growth and inflation with U.S. consumption of a particular food product. Alternatively, an investment adviser might want to see the effect of tight money policies by the Federal Reserve on stock and bond prices, inflation, and economic growth during the 1970s. Or perhaps a new labor relations specialist at a major corporation would like a concise summary of every article written in the United States on labor over the previous five years.

The suppliers of business information are clearly in the catbird seat. Not only is demand for their services increasing, but their cost of doing business — collecting, processing, and disseminating information — is declining rapidly. In the early 1970s IBM was selling computer System 360 for about $250,000. But by 1980 *Intel* was able to produce a computer with the same amount of computing power for $6.50 and sell it for $35.

Technology is helping the industry in another way, too. As electronic hardware systems permeate office and home, it becomes easier and easier to segment markets and provide the specific, relevant information that is needed by any particular segment. Anyone with a video screen will eventually have access to numerous data bases as well as instant access to any specific piece of information.

This ability will be worth a lot to the user because the information that can be packaged and segmented properly acquires greater value. For instance, an annual subscription to *Business Week* magazine costs $34.95, but the value of the information in fifty-two issues, if it were organized and instantly accessible in relevant categories, would be significantly higher. Then McGraw-Hill, the owner of *Business Week,* could resell to others information it already gathered with little additional cost to itself.

Dow Jones is another example of a company that takes existing resources and repackages them in many different forms. The company, for example, compiles the Dow Jones industrial average hourly (or even more frequently) for its electronic services, summarizes the same data in *The Wall Street Journal* and *Barron's* on a daily and weekly basis, and publishes annual compilations of the same statistics. In this case, the relatively high cost of information acquisition and processing is spread over a variety of markets in slightly different formats with comparatively low reproduction costs.

Along the same lines, the data base of a publisher, especially if stored electronically, is of value to the same customers over time. The New York *Times,* which has been developing such an information base for a decade, also offers abstracts of a large number of other publications to its customers.

Another plus for the business information industry is that it increasingly serves smaller and thus more specialized markets. This phenomenon is a result of the explosion in the amount of information, an event which affects us all. There is so much to know, so many new spheres of knowledge, so much activity in so many different fields of study and so many professions that the mind grows numb to think of how quickly one's knowledge decreases in relation to total knowledge.

Several decades ago, someone with a fine brain, a retentive memory, and an interest in learning could assimilate a good portion of what was known. Through judicious reading and observation, such a person could keep up with the developments in most important spheres of human activity.

Today, one faces the horrifying revelation that unless one absorbs a tremendous amount of information, one will actually regress in one's relative understanding of world developments. Yet, each of us can absorb only a certain amount of information. While the total number of magazines might increase, the number of people reading each one cannot. The good news for information companies in all this is that highly specialized information products are of increasing

Table 11

THE BUSINESS INFORMATION INDUSTRY
($ billions)

	1978	1979	1980	1984E	1979 – 84 compound annual growth (%)
Total world revenues	8.05	9.80			
U.S. revenues	7.15	8.70	10.53	22.7	21
Computer revenues	1.00	1.35	1.73	4.5 – 5.7	27 – 33
Computer revenues as a % of total U.S. revenues	13.8	15.5	16.4	20 – 25	

value to subscribers, as well as to those, such as advertisers, who wish to reach the subscribers.

The proof of the good prospects for the information industry can be seen in its growth rate. The Information Industry Association estimates that the industry has been growing at the rate of 20 percent or more a year — and information from computers at 30 percent annually. Table 11 shows the recent revenue growth and the future projections.

A number of companies are focusing their corporate resources on the development of business information and the collection and delivery of that information by electronic means. We have identified a number of such companies that we believe are in the forefront of using the new technologies.

THE COMPANIES

Dow Jones & Co. is the premier company in the area of business and financial information. Heightened business competition, rapidity of change, and a growing national awareness of the importance of developments in the business and financial system all augur well for the company's major markets.

Its leading publication is *The Wall Street Journal,* presently the largest circulation newspaper in the country (nearly 2 million readers), as well as one of the fastest growing (circulation rose 32 percent in the last five years). *The Wall Street Journal* is also very aggressive in its pricing, with both subscription and advertising rate increases jumping at better than a 20 percent annual rate. Circulation also increased at *Barron's,* Dow Jones's financial weekly, and at the company's local newspapers.

Dow Jones is a pioneer in developing and using new technologies, having introduced printing by satellite in 1975. Its manufacturing facilities currently incorporate the most modern equipment and facilities available. A vigorous innovator, the company is presently introducing new products at the rate of about one a month.

Dow Jones has a solid footing in the emerging data-based publishing industry via its computerized news retrieval service for homes and offices. This part of its business should grow rapidly since Dow

Jones owns the world's largest news service — which can now be purchased by owners of Radio Shack personal computers. The company is capitalizing on the favorable outlook for cable TV via acquisitions and the recent launching of a cable financial news service.

Dow Jones is apparently less vulnerable to business downturns, particularly those in the securities industry. Also, *Barron's* and *The Wall Street Journal* are broadening their bases and, now that their news coverage has expanded and features are run on a regular basis, appeal to a wider audience.

Socioeconomic trends should also favor the company in the years ahead. The prime audience for most of the company's publications is the thirty-five-to-fifty-year-old group and households with incomes over $50,000 — both of which are projected as the fastest-growing segment of the population in the 1980s.

Dun & Bradstreet Corp. is evolving into the prototype of the successful financial publisher in the 1980s — a purveyor of information via electronics. D&B was the first publisher to make the major shift from paper files to electronic ones. In the mid-1970s, the company started advanced office systems (AOS), which enabled it both to reduce clerical costs and to expand its product line by restructuring its information. Since the conversion to AOS in 1975, D&B has introduced over twenty major computer-based services and a host of minor ones and has made numerous acquisitions in the software field. The company continues to develop new products and services at a fast pace.

McGraw-Hill, Inc. is one of the largest U.S. publishers of business press publications, trade journals, and college textbooks. A decade ago it was generally identified with one or the other of those fields, but now it has redefined itself as primarily an information company. Today, it is also the largest producer of economic and construction information, as well as one of the two largest sources of financial information and the dominant factor in a host of smaller sectors.

McGraw-Hill should be one of the industry's outstanding performers through the mid-1980s. For one thing, the company has improved its profitability through increased use of new technologies. What's more, it has developed an impressive line of specialty information services including Standard & Poor's, the Dodge Reports, and the recently acquired Data Resources line of economic data bases.

A. C. Nielsen Co. has long regarded itself as an information service company and as such is a perfect example of the evolving nature of publishing. Best known for its TV audience-rating services, its actual core operations involve broader marketing research, particularly the measurement of branded merchandise movement at retail levels.

Its research services activities also include the Media Research Group (TV, cable, and new media); Coordinated Management Systems (on-line computer management information systems); and Dataquest Inc. (comprehensive information on eleven technological and industrial markets).

Its Clearing House Services process the coupons used by many companies to attract consumers. Its Petroleum Information Services utilize the most comprehensive data bank on oil fields and operations in the world.

Among its other services are Neodata, which maintains and processes mailing lists and magazine circulation lists, and Compumark (sales management consulting and automated processing of sales call reports).

Nielsen continues to enhance its services and their profitability by expanding its use of electronics. Its ScanTract Service offers weekly information on merchandise movements garnered from optical scanning of Universal Product Code bars on packaged goods in many of the three thousand-odd outlets with the necessary equipment.

Commerce Clearing House is the largest U.S. publisher of loose leaf material on the subject of taxation and business regulation aimed at professionals. It is also one of the largest computer processors of income tax returns for the clients of these professionals. This is a good area of growth, as you can well imagine. The complexity of government regulation and taxation has increased drastically in recent years. Accordingly, the company has experienced growth from an expansion in the number of services it sells, as well as the numbers of subscribers to its publications.

CHAPTER 8

Factory Electronics

Robots and fully automated factories in the United States have been talked about for years. But now they may finally become a reality. More attractive technology, the end of the baby boom (and the eventual shortage of unskilled labor), the need to modernize or reindustrialize an aging U.S. manufacturing base, pressure to reduce the use of labor that is more expensive than that of most of our international competition, and a more favorable tax structure will lead to increasingly automated factories.

The automated factory has long been a dream of the manufacturing world, and small wonder. The production manager, who is always under pressure to improve output, normally agrees with those classical economists who ranked technological advancement as the most important determinant of productivity, with capital investment and labor a distant second and third.

Part of the present economic problems in the United States stems from the fact that business had to operate in an exceptionally difficult economic environment during most of the 1970s, harassed by rapidly increasing inflation, exploding energy prices, and gyrating money markets. This situation brought about a decade of sluggish economic growth, weak research-and-development spending, and economic policies that favored consumption over investment. As a result, real capital spending trailed significantly behind the strong outlays of the 1960s. As you can see from Table 12, the 1.5 percent annual increase in productivity during 1973 – 79 was half our historic norm. In fact, things were so bad that some economists even suggested labor was the only area that actually boosted productivity growth during the period.

Table 12

THE IMPORTANCE OF CAPITAL SPENDING

	% growth real GNP	% growth real gross private fixed investment	% growth real plant and equipment spending	% growth productivity
1959–72	3.8	4.9	3.8	3.1
1973–79	2.5	2.1	2.1	1.5

The economic environment of the 1970s favored capital outlays that resulted in a quick payback — in other words, machinery rather than bricks and mortar. As a result, the share of U.S. capital spending going for automation rose throughout the 1970s, reaching nearly 40 percent of manufacturing outlays in 1977–78.

However, by the late 1970s the pressure of high interest rates, high inflation, and an uncertain economic outlook began to take their toll on corporate outlays. By the same token, record long-term interest rates and a rapidly expanding work force made labor more attractive than capital investment. Thus, as you can see from Table 13, the share of U.S. capital spending by manufacturers on automation declined sharply, from 39 percent in 1978 to 27.2 percent in 1980.

The 1980s, however, promise to be a period of renewed commitment to factory automation. As Table 13 indicates, spending on automation by all business is estimated to increase to 25.2 percent in 1982, up from 21.5 percent in 1980.

Increased spending on automation will eventually come about because of two trends:

- A more favorable economic environment. As discussed earlier, we expect an abatement in the energy price explosion, continued improvements in the tax structure for business, and meaningful productivity growth from new technology.
- A sharp reversal in demographic trends. The end of the baby boom will cause a sharp drop in the number of people entering

the work force starting in 1984. The unavailability of labor will force the manufacturing world to begin to change its methods of production, leading to a substitution of capital (investment) for labor.

In fact, we expect the U.S. factory to evolve along the same lines as U.S. agriculture. It was the substitution of capital for labor that transformed agriculture from the major employer after the Civil War to a minor one in the 1980s, when it is engaging less than 4 percent of the U.S. work force at present. Capital investment in the factory should also sharply reduce employment and costs in the manufacturing area over the next few decades. We expect that as we head into the twenty-first century, the percent of the work force employed in manufacturing could drop toward 10 percent from the present 28.6 percent. While that may sound extreme, there is no doubt that robots and the truly automated factory are finally achievable.

Table 13

PERCENT OF U.S. CAPITAL SPENDING FOR AUTOMATION[a]

	1978	1980	1981E	1982 (planned)
Electrical machinery	46.0	36.7	39.9	39.9
Machinery	44.0	27.2	38.0	42.2
Auto / truck parts	26.6	15.6	18.2	19.0
Aerospace products	31.1	31.6	30.7	30.5
Fabricated metals	35.1	34.6	35.2	27.0
All metal products	40.6	28.1	32.4	33.7
Total durable goods	NA	27.5	31.6	34.2
Total nondurable goods	NA	26.9	26.5	27.5
All manufacturing	39.0	27.2	29.0	30.7
All business	NA	21.5	23.2	25.2

[a] Sources: McGraw-Hill; *The American Machinist.*

HOW WILL FACTORY AUTOMATION UNFOLD?

If the automated factory of the future is really coming, the critical question becomes how we will get there. We believe that certain trends already in force will be the major focus of manufacturers through mid-decade:

• Modernization of the aging U.S. manufacturing base. Two thirds of all U.S. machine tools (the machines that run industry) are over ten years old and one third are more than twenty years old.

• Increased penetration of electronics (i.e., computer power) into the manufacturing sector. Sales of industrial electronics, which totaled $2.8 billion in 1980 (or 17 percent higher than in 1979), could exceed $5.5 billion by the middle to late 1980s.

Meanwhile, a number of new products are coming on stream that will have important influences on factory automation. Foremost among these are:

• Sophisticated machine tools.

• Electronic hardware that is used to control the sophisticated equipment or to perform other tasks, specifically, programmable controllers (devices that, in effect, marry computer and machine tool), mini- and microcomputers, and robots.

• Computer-aided design (CAD) and computer-aided manufacturing (CAM) systems. These systems generate significant cost savings to an increasing number of industries by raising the productivity of designers and engineers, thereby cutting the product development and manufacturing costs cycle. With a CAD / CAM system, an engineer can sketch, rework, and redraft his design on a small TV-like screen in the same way that a word processor allows continual editing.

• Software. If anything, it will be the lack of software, not hardware, that will slow the advance of sophisticated technology into the manufacturing sector.

But we'd rather not think of the automation industry in terms of existing trends or new products. We think there are better objects to focus on in the industry: the companies that will benefit from trends in the first half of the 1980s and those that will benefit from trends in the second half. During the early part of the 1980s, the prime investment prospects are likely to continue to be those companies that are benefiting from rapid penetration of sophisticated technology into the manufacturing world. In general, these are:

- Machine tool companies, such as *Cincinnati Milacron, Cross & Trecker, Giddings & Lewis,* and *Ex-Cell-O.*
- CAD / CAM companies, such as *Computervision.*
- Minicomputer companies, such as *Digital Equipment* and *Data General.*
- Factory electronics and robot companies. Unfortunately, the major suppliers in these fields are either small divisions of large companies or privately held companies, which leaves little opportunity for investors. For instance, the major companies making programmable controllers are *General Electric* (GE) and *Allen Bradley.* In machine tool controls, it's General Electric, Allen Bradley, Cincinnati Milacron, Warner & Swasey (*Bendix*), Cross & Trecker, and *Square D.* In robots, it's Cincinnati Milacron, *Unimation* (Condec), *Automatix,* GE, *Texas Instruments* and *International Business Machines,* DeVilbiss (*Champion Spark Plug*), Cybotech (joint venture of *Ransburg* and Renault), *Nordson, Advance Robotic Corp.,* and *PRAB.* For factory electronics, it's GE, *Schlumberger, Eaton,* Bendix, *TRW, Litton, Gould,* Square D, and *Exxon Corp.*

During the second half of the 1980s, investment strategy for factory automation may change. By that time we expect the manufacturing sector to begin moving toward a systems approach to factory automation, leading to the automated factory by the end of the century.

On the one hand, it's clear that machine tools, robotics, CAD / CAM, and computer-oriented product lines are the key ingredients to factory automation. But on the other hand, the development of a systems-oriented approach is highly capital-intensive and involves a strong commitment to both electronics and software. This suggests that during the second half of the 1980s, large companies with the necessary financial resources may become key participants in the growth of the automated factory.

To be sure, an analysis of the reallocation of assets of some of the larger U.S. corporations suggests that significant changes in their corporate strategies have already taken place. During the mid-1970s, the explosion of energy prices as well as sluggish economic growth resulted in radical changes in cash flow and growth expectations for various economic sectors:

● Energy related companies serving the oil and oil service sectors were prime beneficiaries of the surge in oil prices as cash flow skyrocketed. As cases in point, Exxon and Schlumberger have attempted through acquisitions to reallocate a portion of their cash flow toward strengthening their electronic and automation capabilities.

● Upward-spiraling energy prices radically changed the growth prospects for transportation-related companies. Truck component manufacturers such as Bendix and Eaton have begun to reallocate their assets through acquisition into growth markets related to automation.

● The higher cost of energy has altered growth prospects for some of the more mundane electrical and power generation equipment. Recognizing this, many larger companies are studying the role they would like to play in the future of automation and have established divisions as a vehicle for participation. GE, for example, has made important acquisitions with a view to improving the position of its automation division.

Although the large companies are likely to play a key role in the factory of the future, potential customers will still require proprietary systems to help them maintain their competitive positions, reinforcing the view that system integration is likely to be a series of joint ventures between large automation companies and their clients' industrial engineering departments and system development groups.

Given the likelihood of a gradual transition into an automation system and the available investment vehicles, the best strategy for the time being is to concentrate one's attention on three major areas: companies that produce the electronics instrumentation that is invading the factory; the machine tool industry; and certain hitherto unglamorous manufacturing companies that are aggressively exploiting the new technology.

ELECTRONICS COMPANIES AND FACTORY AUTOMATION

It is most appropriate to start our discussion of companies well positioned in factory automation with an overview of the electronics industry. The major impetus behind such automation is the electronics invasion of the factory, which is occurring because of the constantly declining cost of computer memory.

The major reason for the decline in the cost of computing power is our ability to put more and more memory functions into a smaller and smaller space. The electronics revolution was really begun in the early 1970s by Intel, a major maker of semiconductors and the creator of the microprocessor, or small computer. According to Gordon Moore, Intel cofounder, the semiconductor industry each year creates as many functions as it previously supplied in its entire history, a synergistic trend which is expected to continue unabated in the 1980s. If the automotive industry had seen the same price / performance improvements of the small-computer industry over the last decade and a half, a Rolls-Royce would now cost $20 and get 10,000 miles per gallon.

As demand for electronics in the factory increases, so will demand for semiconductors. But Japanese competition has made the U.S. industry a relatively unattractive business proposition. However, certain suppliers to the industry could do well.

Take *Teradyne, Inc.,* as a case in point. This company tests the quality of already-made semiconductors for both domestic and foreign companies. Driven by a need for greater product reliability and better utilization of engineering manpower, producers of semiconductors are more and more often turning to computer-based testing systems, an area in which Teradyne occupies a dominant position.

At this writing, the company is generally perceived by the investment community as a cyclical supplier of equipment to the highly cyclical semiconductor industry. This view was correct in 1970 when about 90 percent of the company's sales were to semiconductor companies, but is inaccurate now since more than 50 percent of Teradyne's shipments presently go to industries whose requirements are less cyclical: data processing, communications, office equipment, and defense.

Veeco Instruments is a major factor in power supplies, which are used to attach a semiconductor-based product to a source of electricity. Since nearly every factory runs on electricity, this business would do well in the era of factory automation.

But the real strength of the company is its breakthrough in the manufacture of semiconductors. It has discovered a way to make semiconductors ten times as fast as in the past. For purchasers, this means the same number of semiconductors for one tenth the price, or ten times as many semiconductors for the same price. Thus, the next-generation decline in computer costs is already taking place — at Veeco.

MACHINE TOOLS

Some see the machine tool industry as a cyclical business that goes from feast to famine because of its dependence on business capital spending. There is obviously truth to this, as orders slumped badly in 1982. But we think the long-term nature of the industry may have changed:

• Machine tool makers are prime beneficiaries of the trend toward reindustrialization, the need for improved productivity, and the move toward a more automated factory.

• The traditional cyclicality of the industry has been somewhat tempered by continuing orders from the automotive and aerospace industries, which presently account for 50 percent of industry sales.

• Government policies to stimulate capital formation (such as, for instance, a faster depreciation write-off) could encourage capital investment in machine tools.

• Future sales to the defense industry, which currently account for 4 percent of machine tool orders, are likely to increase because of a renewed commitment to increased military expenditures. This market could grow so significantly that defense could replace the aerospace market in the 1980s as one of the top sources of demand.

• One of the major problems of the machine tool industry, its lack of capacity, is on the way to being solved. During the surges in demand for machine tools, which occurred in 1973 – 74 and

1978–79, domestic manufacturers were unable to meet all of the demand and imports had to take up the slack.

As a result, imports increased more than sixfold during the 1970s and in 1980 accounted for some 25 percent of total U.S. machine tool consumption, as against 10 percent during the early 1970s. We believe this loss of market share would be reversed if the domestic industry were able to guarantee deliveries and meet shorter delivery schedules.

Given the fact that the domestic machine tool industry increased capital spending by 55 percent to $145 million in 1979 and by a similar amount in 1980, total capacity has probably increased as much as 50 percent. That should go a long way toward alleviating the supply problems in the next industry up cycle.

The best positioned company in machine tools is also the largest: *Cincinnati Milacron.* This company's major strategic thrust is to combine electronics and machine tools. It wants to make machine tools more effective and more efficient by adding a computer to a machine tool. If one operator can control three or four machine tools instead of one or two, labor productivity will be greatly increased. Cincinnati Milacron, as we mentioned earlier, is also a major factor in robots and offers a good vehicle for participation in that business.

THE ELECTRONICS REVOLUTION CAN CHANGE THE VERY NATURE OF A COMPANY

Innovative, aggressive users of the new technologies may also be the beneficiaries of the electronics revolution. And indeed, two electrical equipment companies are in the process of a major redeployment of resources away from their old industrial markets into rapidly growing high-technology markets.

Gould Inc., an erstwhile manufacturer of electrical products, batteries, and a diversified list of industrial products, is aggressively selling off these operations. In 1981, for instance, Gould sold its bearings and piston business and a high-voltage electrical equipment venture. Meanwhile, the company has made a number of acquisitions in the electronics business. In 1977 Gould purchased Modicon Corp., a producer of programmable controllers, and in 1980 Systems Engineering Laboratories, a minicomputer company.

Gould hopes to become a major factor in factory automation. It is already the largest producer of programmable controllers, a product that is used to interface the computer and the machine tool. In effect, programmable controllers instruct machine tools to do certain repetitive tasks, almost like robots. Since most machine tools are still unconverted to the new technology, the potential market for programmable controllers is large. Over the longer term, Gould hopes to become the largest supplier of the type of factory automation system that we envision for the future.

Square D is a major producer of switches, circuit breakers, and other electrical devices. As well as making acquisitions in the electronics industry, the company is aggressively developing new electronic products to help industrial productivity, such as programmable controllers and energy management systems. Another plus for Square D is its strong international growth (particularly in Mexico) and the successful relocation of much of its manufacturing operation to the South where it enjoys lower labor costs and less labor unrest.

CHAPTER 9

Energy Producers

It is energy that makes our economy go: energy fuels our transportation system, heats our homes in winter and cools them in summer, produces our goods and our food, lights our offices and houses, fuels our factory and office systems, provides the juice for almost every appliance and convenience in the home from TVs to dishwashers, and in our hospitals, runs the latest medical equipment that performs near-miraculous lifesaving feats. In short, almost everything in our modern industrialized society depends on energy.

Another way of confirming the importance of energy is to count the number of energy giants that exist in our economy. A quick look at the five hundred largest companies in the nation shows that a majority of the top twenty are energy companies. Think also of the great family fortunes of this nation — such as Rockefeller and Hunt — which were founded on oil.

The major energy-producing states are among the richest, most prosperous ones in the United States. And some of the major oil-producing countries in the Middle East have the highest per capita wealth in the world.

Energy is not just another commodity. It is the most important ingredient of any highly sophisticated, complex industrialized nation, and as such, its price and availability is of critical importance to everyone who uses it.

The arguments for a long-term investment in energy are most compelling. In the simplest terms, think of the price of gasoline, which has jumped to more than $1.30 a gallon from around 30 cents in the early 1970s. That higher price hurts consumers, but benefits the companies that have oil to sell.

The energy companies we focus on in this chapter will benefit from three important facts:

1. Because of the vulnerability of Mideast oil, the United States is increasing production of oil and natural gas.
2. Despite recent reductions in oil consumption due to greater conservation, long-term demand for oil and gas is likely to increase. Our economy is too heavily dependent upon these sources of energy for it to be otherwise.
3. The oil industry is experiencing a significant shift in market share as the independents, not the majors, are now spending the greater part of the funds expended on energy development.

THE VULNERABILITY OF OIL SUPPLIES FROM THE MIDDLE EAST

The fall of the Shah of Iran and the Iran-Iraq war, which came with unexpected suddenness, highlighted this country's vulnerability to any political disruption in the Persian Gulf region. Those two events cost the world some 9½ million barrels of oil production daily (out of a total of some 60 million barrels). Needless to say, any additional political or military jolts in that area could wreak untold havoc on Western economies.

Despite some recent improvements, the Mideast is a hotbed of potential political crisis. The Iran-Iraq war, for instance, created a number of long-term changes. First, it altered many of the Arab alliances and weakened the influence of the U.S. in the region. It has also encouraged religious conflict by accentuating the differences between the Sunni and Shiite Moslems. Since the basis of much Iran-Iraq hostility is religious, a complete reconciliation between the two countries appears unlikely; one need only look at the long-standing wars in Lebanon and Northern Ireland to appreciate the difficulty in achieving peace when religion is involved.

Another danger in the energy situation in the West lies in its excessive dependence on Saudi Arabia. As this book is written, Saudi wells are pumping over 20 percent of all the oil produced by non-Communist countries. For the West to rely so heavily on any country, no matter how friendly, is to ask for trouble. The Saudis do not have adequate means of protecting themselves from outside military aggression and since half their population consists of foreign labor, they are vulnerable to political unrest or revolution.

The position of the Soviet Union in the Middle East is certainly stronger than that of the United States. Geographically, the U.S.S.R. is close to the region and undoubtedly would try to exploit any disruption in the area to its advantage.

While the United States may talk at length about defending the Persian Gulf oil fields, as a practical matter there is very little that this country can do. The distances involved, the anti-American feeling in the area, and the explosive worldwide political reaction that would occur at any hint of U.S. military involvement might well preclude us from any direct action — even if we had the forces capable of defending the area, which we do not.

THE LONG-TERM OUTLOOK FOR SUPPLY AND DEMAND

Oil prices dropped sharply in 1982 as the worldwide recession reduced consumption and OPEC pricing began to crumble. In all probability, we have seen the long-term peak in oil prices. How low oil prices will fall before stabilizing is anyone's guess. Back before OPEC controlled prices, deflation (in addition to inflation) in the price of oil was the norm. A big drop in oil prices cannot be ruled out. But over the long term, energy will be necessary for any economic recovery. Accordingly, while energy pricing may not be as attractive as it was in the 1970s, there will be volume opportunities for low-cost producers.

In evaluating the supply / demand situation for oil, one must remember that oil can be held in the ground indefinitely, with no deterioration in quality. Because of oil's durability and storability, oil prices are based as much, if not more, on expected future demand than on present demand. Thus, if the future appears to require high prices to balance supply and demand, then there will be a tendency for current prices to firm up, as the oil producers cut back in anticipation of better prices later on.

What about conservation? Won't that reduce demand even during an economic recovery? While conservation should not be down-played, neither should its potential be overestimated. Energy plays too great a role in the production and consumption of goods in our economy for feasible conservation to make a really major inroad into demand. In a 1980 study the National Academy of Sciences estimated that each 1 percent rise in energy costs reduces long-term energy use by slightly less than ¼ of 1 percent.

What about synthetic fuels and non-OPEC production? Unfortu-nately, there's little cause for optimism here either.

The congressional Office of Technology Assessment recently pre-dicted that the location of worldwide oil reserves will hardly change by the end of the century, with two thirds of the non-Communist world's reserves still located in the Middle East.

Some areas that have potentially vast reserves, such as the Cana-dian Arctic, are not financially attractive at current prices of oil. And other promising areas, like Mexico, will require long and costly development periods before substantial production increases are possible. Finally, even massive exploration efforts in places like the lower forty-eight states will do little more than offset declining do-mestic production. In sum, we see non-OPEC production increasing to no more than 24 million barrels a day (from 1981's 22 million) by 1990.

As for synthetic fuels, they are not economic at current prices. Coal liquefication is not yet economical, and although coal gasifica-tion and synfuel from oil shale may be marginally attractive at cur-rent prices, they are unlikely to be developed fast enough to make much difference in the overall supply / demand situation. (The United States would have to employ 15 percent of its entire con-struction industry on synfuel plant construction in order to produce just 500,000 barrels per day by 1990.)

MARKET-SHARE SHIFT

A massive market-share shift in domestic energy production is presently taking place. Once an economic recovery increases demand

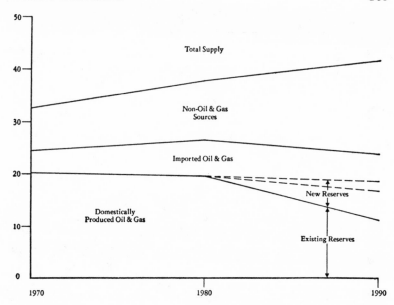

Exhibit 9 – 1
Estimates of U.S. production of oil and natural gas.

for energy, U.S. oil and natural gas production from existing reservoirs could fall by 40 percent or more in the 1980s, as you can see from Exhibit 9 – 1. Just to keep our energy imports down during the 1980s, we will have to find substantial new reserves.

By 1990 the finders and producers of these new reserves could receive between $200 and $300 billion in revenues per year, as shown in Exhibit 9 – 2. However, the bulk of these revenues is not going to be generated by the big oil companies, which, in effect, have left the energy business, preferring to invest their cash flow in minerals, electrical equipment, food retailing, and other ventures.

In fact, the major oil companies are no longer the oil *industry*. Both inside and outside the United States, the major oil companies are playing a smaller and smaller role in oil-field activity. Nonetheless, many investors still use the majors as proxies for oil-field expenditures despite the fact that the twenty-nine largest U.S. oil companies drilled only 12.1 percent of the domestic wells and provided

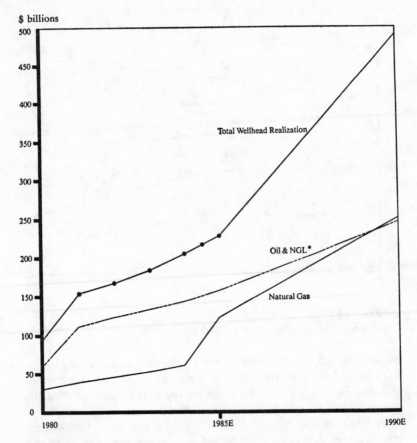

Exhibit 9 – 2
Potential revenues from domestically produced oil and gas.
* Natural Gas Liquids

27.6 percent of the domestic drilling expenditures in 1980. As shown in Table 14, the majors are completing about 2 percent fewer domestic wells per year in comparison to the independents. With the increasing power of national oil companies, such as Pemex in Mexico, major U.S. oil companies are also losing market share in wells drilled outside the United States.

Table 14

**PERCENT OF U.S. OIL WELLS COMPLETED
BY TWENTY-NINE LARGEST U.S. OIL COMPANIES**

Year	Percent
1980	12.1%
1979	13.6
1978	14.9
1977	17.2

The small independent producers are the ones spending the money and are, therefore, the ones most likely to find new reserves and generate the huge increases in revenues we are projecting.

The international oil companies, significantly, depend on OPEC for a major percentage of their oil, while the independents do not. This difference is striking. Take, as a case in point, British Petroleum (BP), one of the largest oil companies in the world. In 1971, BP's oil reserve position was 65 billion barrels. But after the confiscations, nationalizations, and other crises of the past ten years, reported reserves had fallen by 1980 to around 6 billion barrels, including BP's 51 percent ownership of Standard Oil of Ohio.

Furthermore, the independents are less affected by an oil glut than the international or foreign oil companies. If the oil glut gets bad enough, the government would put restrictions on the amount of imported oil coming into the country. This would help to support the domestic energy industry, which has huge investments in high-cost developments such as Alaska's North Slope. However, small companies which took on a lot of debt to acquire leases and explore for oil and gas could be in desperate straits, if the oil glut continues for several years.

Some analysts are skeptical about our ability to reverse the decline in domestic production. We, however, think such skepticism fails to recognize the favorable economics of energy exploration and development. The average finding costs of new energy so far are well below the current market price.

Natural gas is the most promising area for production increases. Many of the smaller companies are exploring for natural gas and finding lots of it. As natural gas prices are decontrolled, even more exploration should take place and production should increase. Many of the natural gas companies discussed in this chapter could generate production volume increases of 200 – 300 percent by the end of the decade.

Furthermore, the industry is getting a host of new drilling prospects. Between 1982 and 1984 the U.S. Government is scheduled to offer more offshore leases to the oil and gas industry than in all the past sixty years put together.

ENERGY PRICING OUTLOOK

We think the oil pricing situation will differ quite markedly in the 1980s from that of the 1970s, as has already been borne out by the drop in the price of oil during 1982. First and foremost, Saudi Arabia realizes that sudden sharp price hikes are enormously disruptive to industrial economies (on which their wealth depends) and must be avoided at all costs. For example, the doubling of oil prices in 1979 – 80 was partly responsible for the ensuing worldwide recession and significantly reduced oil consumption.

If OPEC wants to maximize its long-term revenues, it should institute gradual price rises of about 4 percent a year above the rate of inflation. This is Saudi Arabia's pricing plan, and as long as OPEC holds together, it could be successful.

According to our long-term assessment of supply and demand, this approach makes the most economic sense for consumers and producers alike, and for this reason we suspect it will win widespread support.

The advantage of a gradual increase to consumers is that it will permit economic growth and avoid the sudden price shocks of the 1970s. The advantage to OPEC is that oil revenues will be maximized if real oil prices increase around 4 percent a year. Any percentage smaller than this would not generate a net rise in revenues, as the trade-off between slightly higher prices and reduced consumption would not be favorable. Anything larger than 4 percent would reduce consumption to the point that higher prices would not bring about an increase in revenues.

Accordingly, once the economy recovers and energy demand increases, real increases in oil prices are apt to be very modest. Of course, oil prices could remain depressed for years, which is why we favor natural gas as an investment. Natural gas is still subject to price controls and sells far below oil on an energy-equivalent basis. (The average price of natural gas in 1980 was $1.56 per thousand cubic feet (MCF), which is the equivalent of oil at $9 a barrel.)

Through 1985 natural gas prices will be gradually increased to free-market levels, which means significantly higher revenues for producers of natural gas. To what level will natural gas prices rise? That depends upon where the price of oil bottoms, but perhaps as high as $5 and $6 per thousand cubic feet at least initially. On the free market at this writing, the United States is paying $4.95 per MCF for imported natural gas. Algeria recently increased the price of liquefied natural gas sold to Belgium from $1.33 to $4.84 per MCF and Indonesia signed an agreement to supply Japan with liquefied natural gas at $5.87 per MCF. But the only natural gas in the United States that is not presently subject to price controls is that found below 15,000 feet, which currently sells for around $8 per MCF. The wild card in the deck is that President Reagan may want the decontrol of natural gas prices to be accelerated. (This would not require the difficult process of congressional approval; the Federal Energy Regulatory Commission — FERC — could do it administratively.) Another alternative is for the U.S. Government to widen the definition of natural gas that is exempt from price controls, to include, for example, gas found below 10,000 feet. Since natural gas is priced below oil on a BTU (British thermal unit) basis and because it offers the short-term solution to our energy needs, we expect exploration incentives to be increased.

THE CHEAPEST OIL IN THE WORLD CAN BE FOUND IN THE STOCK MARKET

One way to make money in the stock market is to buy companies whose asset values exceed the price of the stock. While such a strategy may take years to work out, there's often less risk involved and usually the promise of a high return.

Considering underlying asset values, some of the domestic oil- and natural gas-producing companies offer value. At this writing, you can buy companies whose total reserves of oil and gas in the ground are valued at between $3 and $5 a barrel. Typically, reserves in the ground are valued at 50 – 60 percent of the current market price for oil less windfall profit tax. If you assume oil in the ground is worth up to $12.50 a barrel, then you can actually buy oil and gas reserves at a third of the going rate.

Take as a case in point the purchase of Seagram Co.'s U.S. oil and gas properties by the Sun Company Inc. in 1980. To begin with, this was an unusual arrangement because Seagram retained an economic interest in the properties and Sun committed itself to spend $400 million developing the properties, but excluding these considerations, Seagram received approximately $13.50 a barrel for its properties. That was in line with the 50 – 60 percent range, given the price of oil at the time of purchase.

One need not be an expert at mathematics to see the long-term attractions of owning companies whose energy assets can be purchased for $3 – 5 a barrel and sold for up to $12.50 — even if the payoff is several years down the road.

Many of the independent oil and gas companies have now increased their capitalization to the point that institutions are now investing in them. Over the course of this decade, many will no doubt be purchased or liquidated, which means, of course, that the investors will realize the true value of those underlying assets.

Unfortunately, the volatility of the stock market and its short-term focus have diverted attention away from the fact that a lot of long-term capital is being invested in these companies. Besides the Sun Oil purchase, other examples are the acquisition of Houston Oil & Minerals by Tenneco for $1.6 billion; an investment in Supron Energy by Total Petroleum; the purchase of Conoco's interest in Hudson's Bay Oil & Gas by Dome Petroleum; and the takeovers of Conoco and Marathon Oil. Highly conservative bankers are lending the money for these purchases of energy assets, so the bankers must be confident of underlying asset values.

One particularly interesting situation is the arrangement between

Mesa Petroleum and Texaco. According to their agreement, Mesa put 1.9 million unexplored acres into a partnership. In return, it will receive a cash contribution of $150 million to the partnership from Texaco, a 75 percent interest in any discoveries, and certain tax benefits; in addition, Texaco will purchase $150 million in 7 percent-coupon preferred stock of Mesa. (After the first $150 million of partnership money is spent, Mesa must put up 25 percent of any subsequent drilling expenditures. But since it has already received $150 million from the sale of the preferred stock, Mesa's real cash contribution won't start until the partnership has spent $600 million.)

What does this mean to Mesa? First, it has acquired financing for an extensive exploration program at very little cost. Secondly, its unexplored acreage has become much more valuable than investors had thought. One way of analyzing this agreement is to observe that Texaco valued Mesa's unexplored acreage at roughly $315 per acre. (Some services at the time were valuing Mesa's unexplored acreage at $25 an acre — which points up the underevaluation of many of these companies.)

THE COMPANIES

In general, investors should look for companies that are in excellent financial shape without too much debt, are able to spend money on exploration, and have rising domestic oil and gas reserves, good acreage holdings, and the prospect of large gains in production. At the same time, these factors should be largely unrecognized by investors — so that the underlying asset value of the company (its appraised worth per share) considerably exceeds the current price of the stock. The geographical location of a company's acreage holdings and the ability of its management to find oil and gas are also most important investment criteria.

Texas Oil & Gas is mainly engaged in collecting and transporting natural gas in Texas and Oklahoma. The company also explores for and produces natural gas and oil, owns an offshore contract drilling subsidiary that operates thirty drilling rigs, and owns or operates seventeen natural gas liquids plants.

The real key to the company's future is its aggressive exploration program and its ownership of 5.27 million undeveloped acres, the largest holding of any independent petroleum company. (Much of this land was acquired before the explosion in natural gas prices; thus, the company's book value is substantially understated.) More than 45 percent of this acreage is located in the gas-rich basins of Texas and Oklahoma and about 21 percent in Kansas. Obviously, the larger the acreage position a company has, the greater its potential for discovering oil and gas; and despite its already huge acreage, Texas Oil continues to add to its holdings. In fiscal 1980 it acquired properties in Louisiana, Utah, Montana, offshore Texas, California, and Nevada.

The company has been quite successful in its drilling efforts, striking oil or gas 60 percent of the time over the past five years, a track record that betters the industry average by a wide margin. During calendar 1980 Texas Oil ranked tenth among all oil companies (including the majors) in terms of oil wells drilled and third in terms of gas wells drilled.

The company's future outlook is good for the following reasons:

- It will receive substantial benefits from the decontrol of natural gas. Not only will its own production of natural gas and natural gas liquids benefit, but the company will receive higher revenues on the natural gas and natural gas liquids that it gathers and transports.

- The company's large unexplored acreage position, its history of successful exploration efforts, and its positive cash flow and financial position will give it a good shot at increasing production of natural gas.

- The gas gathering and distribution business offers earnings predictability. Texas Oil has a good earnings record, with twenty-three years of earnings growth compounded at an annual rate of 46 percent a year.

Transco Companies owns and operates a natural gas pipeline serving the eastern United States. It is also aggressively exploring for oil and natural gas, primarily in the Gulf Coast area.

Transco would be a major beneficiary of any accelerated decontrol of natural gas. A likely step in this direction, as we mentioned earlier, is decontrol of natural gas found between 10,000 and 15,000 feet. Since 50 percent of Transco's natural gas is located between 10,000 and 15,000 feet, any such action could have an immediate impact on cash flow and earnings.

Transco would also benefit more than most companies from total decontrol. Many natural gas producers have substantial portions (between 30 and 50 percent) of their natural gas production committed under long-term contracts. By contrast, less than 10 percent of Transco's production is committed under such contracts.

Transco's pipeline earnings provide a good source of cash flow for the company's successful exploration program. At this writing, Transco is devoting 25 percent of its exploration efforts to locating gas below 15,000 feet, a strategy which is further enhancing cash flow.

Freeport-McMoRan, Inc. is a unique company with interests in a number of important businesses. The company is the result of a recent merger between Freeport Minerals Co. and McMoRan Oil & Gas Co., an aggressive oil and gas exploration company.

The combined company is now a major factor in sulfur and phosphate fertilizers and in copper, in addition to its fast-growing energy business. In recent years, the United States has had relatively good weather and our bumper harvests have postponed possible world food shortages that face us as worldwide population growth continues to exceed food production. But if and when agricultural commodities begin to rise again, the fertilizer business would be a major beneficiary. Although copper is depressed at this writing, its long-term picture may eventually improve. Little new capacity has come on stream in recent years, and there's no incentive to add any since copper prices are way below the cost of production. Rising demand and dwindling supplies could eventually force copper prices higher.

Freeport also produces 30 billion cubic feet of natural gas a year, from which the company could benefit if there is decontrol. Some 25 billion cubic feet of this gas is produced from below 10,000 – 15,000 feet and is therefore likely to be freed from controls in the near future.

Woods Petroleum is exploring for oil and natural gas primarily in the Anadarko Basin, in Oklahoma, and the Rocky Mountains, two of the most promising areas in the whole country. The company's major emphasis at this writing is on natural gas found below 15,000 feet. Woods runs one of the best oil / gas limited drilling partnerships — which gives the company increased exploration leverage. Its accounting practices are among the most conservative of the small independent companies. Woods also has acreage in certain promising regions in Alberta, Canada and Indonesia.

May Petroleum is one of the fastest-growing exploration companies in the industry. For the five years ending in 1980, May's oil and gas reserves grew at a better than 50 percent rate, while earnings jumped 65 percent. Historically, May has relied mainly on drilling funds to finance its exploration program, but recently it has shifted toward self-financing, as well as toward higher-risk projects.

May has a 1.2 million-acre position in the western United States, largely in the booming Overthrust Belt. Given the size of the acreage and its location, the company has a chance of achieving a significant increase in reserve position.

Universal Resources Corp. is a small exploration company that operates mainly in Oklahoma, the Rocky Mountains, North Dakota, Wyoming, and Texas. Its strategy can best be described as a moderate-risk, widely dispersed approach. The company typically takes a 5 – 25 percent share in expensive, high-risk projects such as the Anadarko Basin development, but as much as 50 – 100 percent of lower-risk, less expensive ventures like the Williston Basin, in North Dakota. In this way, the company adds reserves on a steady, predictable basis — without putting everything on any one prospect.

The real attraction of Universal Resources is its exploration effort in the deep Anadarko Basin. Assuming only moderate success in this area, the company could add as much as 150 billion cubic feet to its natural gas reserves by 1985 — almost triple its 1981 stated reserves.

Niklos Oil & Gas Co. is a small exploration company operating primarily in southern Louisiana. The company's aggressive exploration program may locate significant reserves and cause a shift in the company's earnings from contract drilling (80 percent of operating income in 1981) to oil and gas production. Niklos is looking for high-risk / reward prospects, the "elephant" finds which could have a massive impact on the revenues of such a small company.

To those living in Colorado, the *Davis Oil Co.* has a special magic all its own. Back in the 1950s and 1960s, when domestic drilling was falling off, Marvin Davis was signing up leases all over the

Rocky Mountains. In recent years Davis has drilled more wells in the United States than anyone else. But Davis's operations are privately held, and thus, don't allow public participation in his exploration efforts.

One good alternative, though, is *Tom Brown, Inc.,* an old independent operator with some of the same wildcatting skills of the Davis Oil Company. Tom Brown, the president of the company, has a long history in the oil business and is drilling in most of the major promising areas in the country — the Overthrust Belt, southern Louisiana, and the Anadarko Basin. He is in the process of converting his company from an independent drilling contractor to a major exploration and production company.

CHAPTER 10

Energy Services

The same developments that make the domestic oil and gas exploration and producing companies attractive on a long-term basis also bolster the position of oil service companies, whose function is to provide drilling and oil-field services to the oil and gas industry.

Naturally, the fundamentals of the oil service industry, like the economics of looking for new reserves, relate directly to the profit picture of the oil and gas industry. The oil glut has severely impacted the profits of oil and gas companies and the oil drilling business. But when the recession ends and demand for energy increases, the oil service business should recover.

Let's look at some of the specific positives for the industry:

1. For one thing, capital will continue to flow into U.S. drilling. Domestic oil and gas revenues at the wellhead level are likely to increase threefold between 1980 and 1986, as projected in Table 15. Wellhead revenues are important determinants of oil service expenditures, and such a dramatic surge in revenues should have a corresponding impact on drilling activity.

2. Drilling attention will focus increasingly on natural gas, which at an average price of $1.50 in 1980 was less than one third of the BTU equivalent of the free market price of oil. Natural gas is scheduled to become totally decontrolled by 1985, but as we've said before, the schedule could be accelerated by President Reagan. Immediate decontrol of natural gas would create as much as $90 billion in wellhead revenues for the industry — which is close to what total oil *and* gas wellhead revenues were in 1980.

Exploration for natural gas will increase even if decontrol isn't accelerated. (Looking for natural gas is a relatively recent phenome-

Table 15

PROJECTED U.S. GROSS WELLHEAD REALIZATIONS COMPARED WITH DRILLING EXPENDITURES

	1	2	3	4
	Oil and NGL^a wellhead realization ($ millions)	*Natural gas wellhead realization ($ millions)*	*Total wellhead realization ($ millions)*	*Drilling expenditures ($ millions)*
1971	11,693	4,097	15,790	2,371
1972	11,707	4,186	15,893	2,814
1973	13,058	4,894	17,952	3,075
1974	21,581	6,573	28,154	4,367
1975	23,116	8,945	32,061	6,571
1976	24,230	11,572	35,802	7,462
1977	25,791	15,825	41,671	9,956
1978	28,478	18,085	46,563	13,061
1979	39,368	24,115	63,483	16,079
1980	67,933	29,956	97,889	22,918
1986E	161,000	132,750	293,800	105,574

^a Natural gas liquids.

non; traditionally, natural gas was regarded as an expendable by-product of oil and there was little economic incentive to find it domestically.) With the passage of the Natural Gas Policy Act of 1978 (which gradually decontrols gas through 1985), the incentive for exploration should improve each year. Of course, most of the natural gas drilling now is taking place in the expectation that the price of gas — and the rate of investment return — could triple within the next three years.

Exploration would also increase if demand for natural gas in-creased — which would happen if the U.S. Government reversed its restrictions on the use of natural gas and forced conversion to other fuels.

This trend toward increased natural gas exploration is positive for the oil service industry. The average natural gas well is deeper (and more costly) than the average oil well.

3. Demand will rise and so will the price of their service. As shown in Exhibit 10 – 1, we expect the increasing value of oil services to result in drilling costs rising faster than actual footage drilled.

Profit margins will be likely to increase during this period.

Rig productivity should increase; new rigs, more productive than

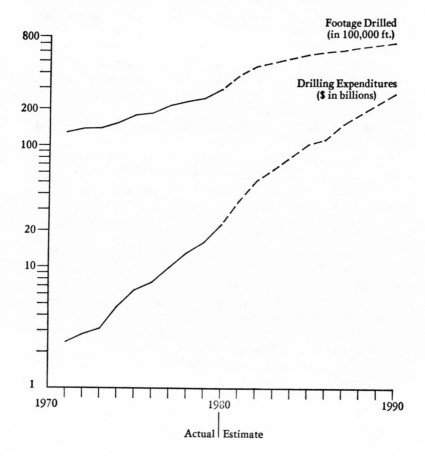

Exhibit 10 – 1
Rising value of oil service business and footage drilled.

older ones, are being added at record rates. This will improve the average productivity of the whole U.S. rig fleet. (Deeper average well depths should only slightly counter the rigs' improved efficiency.)

4. A relatively stable political environment, as well as oil decontrol, has attracted much of the worldwide drilling activity to the U.S. Meanwhile, the political situation is less and less attractive in other countries. In the North Sea, for instance, oil companies are experiencing frequent increases in British tax rates on oil production. Canada's proposal to take over much of the foreign-owned oil industry has caused a mass exodus of non-Canadian drilling activity and expenditures. The result is that some 80 percent of the oil wells now being drilled in the world are located in the United States. Policies in Britain and Canada may change, but in the meantime the United States has picked up a permanent gain in share of world drilling funds.

In fact, the relationship between the U.S. Government and the domestic oil and gas industry is the best it's been in years. U.S. oilmen believe that the government finally supports their efforts to increase production. This gives the whole industry an important psychological boost and raises the odds that oilmen will take the great financial risks involved in searching out new supplies.

5. The economics of drilling for oil and gas — the most important factor — is good. The Independent Petroleum Association of America estimates that the cost of finding oil is currently $10 – 12 a barrel. Thus, after adjusting for the windfall profits tax, an investment in a successful U.S. oil well can return 100 percent per year. Furthermore, because of the need to reduce imports of foreign oil, any domestic oil that is found can be sold.

In fact, the economics of domestic oil exploration is now so attractive that capital is flowing in from outside sources. For example, the number of independent oil companies has soared from 4,793 in 1974 to 8,687 in 1980. Even traditionally conservative institutional investors are investing directly in the oil and gas business.

6. The major oil companies will continue to invest money in domestic exploration activities. These companies have largely been cut off from their sources in the Middle East and frequently find themselves in competition with their former suppliers. In order to replace the loss of this supply, the majors will probably reinvest a much

higher percentage of wellhead revenues in domestic drilling than in the past. Furthermore, if external financing is necessary, the oil companies will have access to capital markets; their balance sheets are underleveraged relative to other U.S. industries, which allows them leeway for additional debt financing.

7. Foreign state-owned oil companies are playing a greater role in worldwide oil drilling. In the countries that have their own oil reserves, the governments are using part of their oil export revenues to finance further exploration activities.

The countries that don't have much domestic production have formed state-owned oil companies out of desperation. Because of balance-of-payments problems and the burden of foreign debts, it's attractive to explore domestically even if the cost of finding oil exceeds imported oil prices.

The emergence of state-owned oil companies is a big plus for the oil service industry because they tend to lack technical expertise and are therefore much more dependent on the service companies than are the major oil companies.

8. An investment in the oil service industry is a form of insurance against Mideast wars, oil shutoffs, or other turmoil. Since any such event would wreak havoc on almost every other investment, oil service stocks are a nice hedge against disaster.

Oil service companies are also mobile — rigs can be moved out of countries seeking control of assets in the ground. And even after the assets are nationalized, the state-owned companies will continue to need oil service companies. Finally, the U.S. oil service industry faces little foreign competition in its more proprietary sectors.

THE COMPANIES

Schlumberger Ltd. is the world's largest oil service company. It is a major land and offshore drilling contractor and the dominant factor in its major markets.

But Schlumberger has become much more than an oil service company by entering the fields of energy management systems, semiconductors, semiconductor testing, and instruments and the use of the new technologies to aid in the exploration for oil and gas. In a sense, the company exemplifies a number of the themes in this book: it is a beneficiary of the higher price of oil, it is exploiting the new technology, and it has redeployed resources into the high-growth electronics business.

Noble Affiliates, Inc., is generally regarded as one of the best contract drillers in the industry, operating a fleet of forty-nine drilling rigs with three more units on order.

Noble is also aggressively exploring for oil and natural gas, with a major emphasis on the Gulf Coast and the Rocky Mountains. Another company that is using the cash flow from one business to finance opportunities elsewhere, Noble is redirecting a part of its cash flow from the contract drilling business into exploration. This, in combination with a large acreage position, gives the company a good shot at significantly increasing its reserve position.

The Western Co. of North America is primarily engaged in offshore drilling and oil and gas pumping services. Its overall strategy is to avoid manufacturing and low value added service operations in favor of proprietary services with high gross profit margins. Although offshore drilling is a good business, the company believes it is not as proprietary as pumping services. Accordingly, an increasing portion of the company's resources will be devoted to the latter area.

Pumping services grew at a nearly 30 percent rate for the five years through 1981 and the industry appears to be very well positioned for the rest of the 1980s. In fact, we believe the pumping services market will be a prime beneficiary of two important oil-field trends we see developing in the United States:

• An increase in natural gas drilling, especially in tight gas sands — gas locked in very small formations. The gradual decontrol of natural gas prices, particularly in tight sands gas formations, has had a positive impact on the stimulation market. (Well stimulation is a way of increasing production of oil and gas by pumping fluids under high pressure inside the well.) *Oil Daily* has estimated that up to 500 trillion cubic feet of new tight gas, representing more than double current U.S. total reserves, could be recovered domestically with full decontrol. Development of these reserves could represent a major market for stimulation services throughout the balance of the century.

- An increase in activity in the potentially more lucrative work-over and recompletion market. In the mid-1970s, new well drilling represented only 60 – 70 percent of pumping services revenues. Work-overs have clearly taken a back seat to new well drilling as oil price controls on older wells skewed the capital commitment toward new wells, but with the decontrol of older oil, the incentive to work over those wells may play an increasing role in the stimulation market in the years ahead. While investors focused attention on the nearly 80,000 new wells that were drilled in 1981, which should generate 80 percent of pumping service revenues, they have (partially) ignored the potential of the 700,000 producing wells which today generate only 20 percent of revenues. Industry observers believe that at least 60 percent of those wells are candidates for major work-overs. A relatively small pickup in work-over activity could produce a sharp increase in total pumping service revenue.

The Western Company has been increasing its market share in the pumping services business by focusing on those parts of the country where pumping is most likely to increase.

Geosource, Inc. is a rapidly growing, high-technology oil service company. Geosource is a major factor in geophysical or seismic surveys, which gather and interpret data about the geological formations of an area, analyzing its potential for oil or gas. Although both geologists and sophisticated equipment are needed to conduct these surveys, Geosource's competitors offer either the geologist or the equipment; Geosource is the only service company that offers both, a major competitive advantage.

Geophysical products and services have been one of the fastest-growing segments of the oil service industry, a trend likely to continue. For one thing, the higher price of oil makes it more economical than ever before to explore remote areas — the more inaccessible a location, the higher the drilling costs, so it makes a lot of sense to do some seismic work before committing huge sums of money. For another thing, the cost of drilling, no matter where it's done, has risen substantially. Thus, dollars spent on preliminary seismic work can prevent money being wasted in fruitless exploration work.

Hughes Tool, the flagship company for the late Howard Hughes, is the world's leading producer of drill bits (with an estimated 40 percent of the world market). The company also manufactures oil and gas production equipment, drilling fluids, and equipment for the construction and mining industry.

Drill bits are perhaps the most basic tools of the drilling business for they actually drill the well. Bits generally have steel cutting teeth, except for drilling very hard rock formations, where tungsten carbide teeth are employed.

The drill bit business would be a prime beneficiary of any worldwide boom in drilling activity. Companies in this business tend to set the cost of a drill bit according to the overall cost of drilling a well. Thus, the drill bit companies will profit from inflation in the oil fields, as well as from any unexpected surge in demand for drill bits.

NL Industries, formerly National Lead, another example of a company that has redeployed its assets into growing businesses, used to produce Dutch Boy paints a number of years ago, but sold out and entered the oil service business. Now it is one of the five largest oil service companies and a major factor in production of "drilling mud," which is used to lubricate the drilling process, cleaning and cooling the hole, and preventing blowouts that might occur at high temperatures.

Drilling mud and other similar fluids are now recognized as among the major elements involved in the success of a drilling operation. A complex mixture of materials and chemicals engineered to meet the requirements of modern rotary drilling, drilling mud is supposed to keep the hole free of cuttings, overcome gas, oil, and water flows, prevent the walls of the well from caving in, and cool and lubricate the drill string. Drilling mud should also permit the maximum information to be obtained from the well by preserving its reservoir characteristics for analysis.

Four major companies dominate the worldwide drilling fluids markets. These are: Magcobar, a division of *Dresser Industries;* Baroid, a division of NL Industries; IMCO, a division of *Halliburton;* and Milchem, a division of *Baker International.* Each company offers a full product line (the minerals barite and bentonite, various chemicals, lost circulation materials, and other specialized items), maintains widely dispersed supply bases, and provides technical support and field engineering. Usually all four companies will be found side by side competing for business in any proven or new oil area.

Together they represent 75 percent of total world sales in drilling fluids, and their unconsolidated joint ventures bring this total closer to 90 percent.

NL's product mix is particularly well situated to benefit from the growing trend toward deep drilling. What's more, the company has been increasing its market share in nearly every one of its major business products. At this writing, the company's depth of market share and technology is not fully appreciated by the investment community.

CHAPTER 11

Deregulation of Transportation

Transportation of goods is something most of us take for granted. But when it breaks down or fails to operate at peak efficiency, our lives are disturbingly disrupted. All things considered, the U.S. transportation system is truly a marvel of efficiency. People, food, machinery, packaged goods, heavy equipment, coal, oil, grain — indeed ourselves and all things our society depends on — are transported over enormous distances and to even the smallest community.

But the system is also amazingly fragile. A trucker's strike, a shortage of oil, a mechanical breakdown in the rail system, delays in air travel due to poor weather, and droughts which affect the barge system can all have devastating effects on the availability of goods and services, inflation and productivity in the economy.

Most strikingly, the higher price of oil is causing a dramatic reevaluation of the way in which goods are transported and, to a certain extent, has affected passenger travel. Shippers all over the country are looking for ways to control transportation costs, and the various segments of the transportation industry — railroads, trucking firms, air freight companies, and airlines — are looking at the economics of their business in light of long-term energy trends, most particularly the relative cost of the various fuels they use. Exhibit 11–1 shows how the cost of freight transportation has soared in the past decade, as well as how the relative price of rail transport has improved versus air or truck transport.

By the year 1990 the U.S. transportation / distribution system will be vastly different from what it is today. The pre-1980 system was founded on cheap and abundant liquid energy and was characterized by tight regulation. Both of these fundamental conditions are now

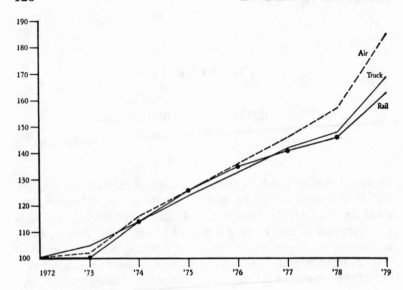

Exhibit 11 – 1
True relative cost of transportation.

changing rapidly, creating a new competitive environment with dramatic opportunities for some companies and causing serious problems, perhaps even extinction, for others.

Deregulation is creating opportunities for three types of transportation entities:

● *Start-ups:* The lower cost structure of a new business can compete effectively against established majors burdened by heavy overheads.

● *Specialized carriers:* Those companies that go after a particular market are finding good growth prospects.

● *Conglomerates:* The company which offers a full range of services is likely to fare well.

There are already numerous signs of the changing times, one of the most visible of which is the start-up of small airlines, such as People Express and New York Air, which offer low-cost air fares. The advent of these new airlines is a direct result of deregulation of the transportation industry, which is removing the barrier to competition and innovation.

Taking a long view, what is the wave of the future? In a word, the answer is "intermodalism," the merging of various transportation forms, such as rail and truck. It will come about, and eventually reign supreme, because of the industry's need to control costs and find the most efficient way to transport goods.

To adapt, however, will require a lot of capital; the big freight transportation conglomerates offering rail, truck, even airline service will need vast amounts of money to take full advantage of all the possible cost saving efficiencies. In effect, these conglomerates will have to enter a number of new businesses and the costs will be substantial.

To appreciate fully the magnitude of the changes that lie ahead one must have an overview of the evolution of the transportation industry up to the present. As you know, the railroad was the first "modern" form of land transportation and it dominated both passenger and freight markets in the late 1800s.

However, the railroad companies' success, and especially their abuses of their power and dominance, bred a severe public reaction against them. This resulted, in 1887, in the first transportation regulation by the U.S. Government, with the Interstate Commerce Act. This act was designed to prevent monopolistic abuses of power, and it was punitive and antirailroad in approach.

The next great period of transportation regulation came during the New Deal days of the 1930s, when the trucking industry, desperately struggling to survive in the depressed business conditions, fought for protective regulation. But when regulation came, it was based on a faulty premise — that economic principles for trucks and railroads are the same.

Unfortunately for the railroads, there is a substantial difference, since trucks have much greater flexibility and lower capital entry costs than do railroads. The inequitable working of the regulation was a major reason why railroads lost a lot of freight traffic to the truckers over much of the post-World War II period.

Further contributing to market share loss by the railroads was the development of the interstate highway system, which encouraged decentralization of the population. That, in turn, favored truckers over railroads because little rail service was available in the new, growing suburban areas.

Airline companies also began to be regulated late in the 1930s. The goal of their regulation was to ensure public safety by encouraging the development of financially stable airlines capable of buying and maintaining safe fleets of aircraft.

But by the 1970s the winds of change were blowing on the periphery of the transportation industry. The first major jolt was a tenfold increase in energy prices and concern over the future availability and price of fuel supplies.

The second major change, which took effect in the late 1970s, was the dismantling of much of the industry regulation. The bankruptcy of the Penn Central railroad company in 1970 and the near-collapse of all the railroad systems in the Northeast and Middle West forced government planners and legislators to reexamine the regulation and makeup of the whole transportation industry.

Legislation to create Conrail out of the ashes of the Penn Central was followed by the Railroad Revitalization and Regulatory Reform Act in 1976. The air freight industry was deregulated in 1977, allowing new competition and competitive pricing. The airline industry was officially deregulated in 1978, although the process was begun earlier by the Civil Aeronautics Board (CAB).

A VISION OF THE FUTURE

Deregulation and the high price of energy — what do they mean to the transportation industry in the United States? How will they affect investments and what are the companies most likely to succeed? Let's start by making some assumptions about the future.

First, regulation of the transportation industry will diminish. In effect, the barriers to competition between the various forms of transportation will disappear in the face of an overpowering need to create a more energy-efficient distribution system.

The 1980s will probably be a period where inefficiencies in all areas of business will become too costly for it to support and will be harshly rooted out. There will be a great deal of corporate restructuring and many traditional industries may actually go through a period of contraction.

New industries based on the latest energy-saving, information-processing, and communications technologies will emerge with different distribution needs. Most probably, their shipments will be small and of high value.

In this environment, there will be numerous opportunities — and risks — for both investors and businessmen. To begin with, freight transportation is going to remain expensive because of high energy costs. What's more, current sophisticated shipping distribution systems will have to be redesigned, with more emphasis on reducing the rate of acceleration of transportation costs.

The best way for business to achieve this is through intermodal operations, which can hold down distribution costs by combining the short-haul (under four hundred miles) flexibility of the truck with the long-haul efficiencies of the railroad. (Railroads now appear to be the most energy-efficient form of transportation,* and each time fuel prices increase, their relative advantage is enhanced.)

Intermodalism for land transportation is already in the works. Freight carriers are being designed for both rail and highway use — the Roadrailer, for example, is a forty-foot highway trailer with both steel wheels for the rails and rubber wheels for the highway. It offers significant productivity savings over "piggybacking" (putting a trailer or container on a rail car). The Roadrailer has gotten regulatory approval and will begin to see service over the next few years.

Federal Express, one of the top air freight forwarders, has substituted trucking for air in Texas and North Carolina, hoping to improve pretax profits by $1 million a year. Consolidated Freightways, a major trucking firm, is using the railroads, as well as handling business for an air freight company. And Missouri Pacific, a major railroad, is aggressively seeking trucking business for its piggyback operations.

The speed with which intermodalism develops will depend on the ability of companies to raise capital to purchase equipment that can

* A recent study for the National Science Foundation found that railroads use 670 BTUs per ton-mile compared to 2800 BTUs for trucks and 42,000 BTUs for air cargo.

achieve maximum energy efficiencies; capital will become critical to success as large conglomerates are formed and compete against the more limited capital resources of their smaller competitors. We can see this already in the airline industry, where ability to purchase the latest fuel-efficient airplane will prove to be a big factor in future profitability.

THE RAILROADS WILL RECAPTURE LOST MARKET SHARE

One definite consequence of higher energy costs will be the U.S. railroads' recapture of a lot of the market share they have lost over the last thirty years. Many railroads could well grow two to three times as fast as the overall economy. Here's the rationale:

• Railroads should be the operating core of the emerging transportation conglomerates because they provide the most energy-efficient way of moving large loads into cities.

• The increased need to transport commodities like coal and grain over long distances will benefit the railroads. Coal is sure to play a part in the nation's becoming less dependent on outside energy sources, and the production of it must increase in the future. Increased production and export of grain will also occur, if forecasts of world food shortages in the mid-1980s prove accurate.

• Railroads are likely to get an increased share of general merchandise freight as piggybacking accelerates. Furthermore, railroads will totally dominate certain long-haul routes, such as Chicago – Los Angeles, because they are so much cheaper. (For example, a Santa Fe piggyback train with one hundred trailers on fifty flatcars pulled by four locomotives uses 18,765 gallons of fuel over the fifty-two hours it takes to go from Chicago to Los Angeles. One hundred tractor trailers going by interstate highway the same 2,100 miles would use 27,000 gallons in fifty-four hours.)

• Poor interconnecting rail service, a major reason for rail traffic problems, may be largely offset by intermodalism. Now, the railroads can use local trucking as an extension of the railroad in areas where connecting rail service is poor. One region that could benefit from intermodalism is the northeastern United States, where

Conrail's inefficiencies have caused connecting railroads to suffer service problems, resulting in traffic losses.

• Railroads will also benefit from the elimination or abandonment of many miles of underutilized track and the absorption of the profitable operations of weaker railroads by the strong ones, which will increase efficiencies. This trend is accelerating and by 1985 should have accelerated to the point that only seven major railroads remain. These railroads should offer improved service and be financially stronger and more profitable than their predecessors.

• Growth in rail revenues will come from an increase in ton-miles (the amount of weight carried multiplied by the number of miles transported), stemming partially from economic growth (once the economy recovers) and partially from greater transportation of bulk commodities such as coal, grain, and chemicals.

This will give the railroads more earnings stability since bulk commodities are less cyclical and not as tied to the level of economic activity. Freight rates should at least equal the rate of inflation over the period because the Interstate Commerce Commission (ICC) plans to index rail rates to the rate of inflation.

• The railroads will continue to work on eliminating inefficiency, improving service, and exercising new rate-making powers. Thus, the compound growth rates in net income for the rails should be 3 to 5 percentage points higher in the 1980s than in the 1970s.

THE COMPANIES

Union Pacific represents the highest-quality investment, not only among railroad stocks, but in transportation stocks generally. It operates in one of the most viable geographical locations, providing the most direct route from the Middle West to the West Coast. It also has the financial and operational capability of adding to both the eastern and western ends of its system.

Perhaps even more important for Union Pacific, besides its strong energy and natural resource position (large oil, gas, and coal reserves), is its proposed merger with Missouri Pacific. Missouri Pacific is in the vanguard of modern railroads, equipped with all of the latest computerized control and information systems. Its territory — from the Gulf Coast, Texas, and Mexico to the industrial

Great Lakes — consists of the fastest growing market in the country. It also can look forward to an expected boom in Mexican traffic, for as Mexico's oil reserves are further developed, traffic between Mexico and the United States will likely increase. Missouri Pacific already has extensive connections with Mexican railroads and will likely be the major beneficiary of this future traffic.

Southern Railway's motto should be "Southern controls the South" rather than "Southern serves the South." Southern Railway, an aggressive developer of intermodal services, should enter the trucking industry quickly, once the law allows it. The combination of an above-average regional growth rate, the strongest marketing department of any railroad, advanced operational control systems, and relatively weak regional competition gives the company an important edge. Southern's aggressiveness and vision of the future could make it the first transportation conglomerate of the 1980s.

TWENTY-FOUR-HOUR AIR FREIGHT SERVICE: THE BIRTH OF A NEW INDUSTRY

Before Xerox copying became ubiquitous, few people perceived a need for copying capability. With its new copier, Xerox Corporation in effect created a market and in doing so generated explosive growth for itself and a whole new industry until the market's appetite was satisfied.

The country is in the midst of another such industry birth — twenty-four-hour air freight service, best exemplified by *Federal Express* and *Purolator*. Before this service was available, most people didn't think there was any great need to get a package or letter to someone within twenty-four hours. But now that the service is available, there is a surprisingly strong demand: a person might need to get a business letter, check, contract, book, or promotional material to an important client or friend as soon as possible; or perhaps, a son wants his father to get a gift in time for an important birthday.

The growth of the small-package market stems from the continuing deterioration of the U.S. Postal Service, the deregulation of the trucking industry (which hampered expansion), the extension of the air service geographically and attraction of new customers, the rapid growth in the need for high-technology companies to get their products to customers with a minimum of delay, and the growing demand for guaranteed overnight delivery.

In the future, success in the industry will rest heavily on the acquisition of fuel-efficient aircraft which can help gain market share (through price reductions) or increase earnings (for buying assets, etc.). The latest information systems, which can help reduce costs further, will also be important to success.

A company must also have the volume to support larger fuel-efficient airplanes and the capital to pay for them. The elimination of regulation is permitting the substitution of trucks for airplanes in many areas. This means fewer flights — but increased shipping volume per flight. Thus, the air freight company with sufficient volume can employ larger aircraft that tend to be more fuel-efficient and cost-effective.

As a result of the burgeoning market, Federal Express could be the fastest-growing air freight company in the United States. Even with its explosive growth to date, the company still has less than 1 percent of the total air freight market.

Federal Express clearly dominates the small-package market and maintains sufficient volume to make economical the larger fuel-efficient aircraft. That, in turn, continues to reduce the average cost per package, which in turn, allows the company to increase its market share and outspend its competition on advertising.

Management at Federal Express is excellent. Its managers are successful entrepreneurs who have taken the company from a start-up operation to a large, professionally managed business. Today the company is the most sophisticated user of new technology of any freight transportation company and has an almost fanatical desire to control costs and boost productivity.

The other well-positioned company in the business is Purolator, Inc. While Federal Express concentrates its efforts on deliveries over four hundred miles, Purolator focuses on packages going less than four hundred miles. Since neither can compete effectively in the other's domain, they are not likely to become direct competitors. Like Federal Express, Purolator has only a small share of the total air freight market, which offers a lot of room for good growth.

POCKETS OF GROWTH IN THE TRUCKING INDUSTRY

The trucking industry has been the most rapidly growing segment of surface transportation over the past three decades. The reasons for this growth have been the suburbanization of the population due to the automobile; the development of the highway system and low-cost energy; the decentralization of industry which followed population growth trends; and manufacturers' need to distribute their centrally made products to anywhere in the country.

Another reason, as we discussed earlier, was that truckers gained a market share from the railroads, which were unable to provide the truckers' flexible service. For example, much of the growth of the nation's economy during the same period occurred in "new" industries that manufactured small, highly valued goods which they had to ship in small quantities to many locations; that favored the truckers over the railroads.

Furthermore, regulation has in general protected the trucking industry from ruinous competition and has encouraged new mergers and acquisitions. Additionally, larger trucks and improved interstate highways boosted trucker productivity, and hence kept a damper on costs.

But in the 1980s the trucking industry will face more negative changes than any other part of the transportation industry. To begin with the industry has minimum potential to produce meaningful productivity savings — so rising costs must be passed along. Also, there's no federal program in the wings comparable to the building of the interstate highway system, which allowed significant service and productivity gains. If anything, continued maintenance of the existing highway system may be inadequate. Finally, deregulation is encouraging more competition (especially from nontraditional sources).

These changes do not threaten the viability of the trucking industry — there is no substitute for the truck in the goods distribution scheme. However, trucks will be used more to pick up and deliver freight within cities or regions than to make long hauls or serve those areas where there is a lot of competition and / or rail service.

Some trucking companies will benefit from these changes and others will suffer. Those that come out ahead must have the ability to control large volumes of freight between regions. This means the companies must be able to pick up, deliver, and consolidate shipments at centralized points, then team up with other shippers to get sufficient volume to reduce costs. Also important will be their ability to finance and participate in joint-venture intermodal projects such as flatcars, piggyback facilities, and trailers. Finally, truckers will need to fill a variety of shipper service needs, from overnight delivery to large-volume movements to warehousing.

Ryder System, Inc. is a prime beneficiary of trucking deregulation. It is a diversified transportation / distribution company whose main business function is to help shippers develop more cost-effective distribution systems. Ryder is also the best-positioned of the distribution service companies, with the dominant position in the most attractive segment of the industry: full-service truck leasing.

In the new deregulated environment, Ryder is gaining market share through an innovative strategy. Having long been a carrier of automobiles, Ryder is expert at dealing with large corporations and anticipating their needs. While most freight forwarders wait for the business to come to them, Ryder is aggressively seeking out large corporations in an effort to win all their transportation business.

Not only did Ryder start from a strong market position, but it has the management and financial resources to thrive in the era of deregulation.

AIRLINES: TAKE-OFF TIME?

The passenger segment of transportation is also expected to change during the 1980s — for many of the same reasons that we have already talked about with regard to freight carriers. In fact, many of the changes in passenger travel are already well under way: greater use of public transportation for commuting; burgeoning demand for smaller, more fuel-efficient automobiles; increases in intercity rail and bus ridership; and less automobile usage. These trends suggest strong demand for buses, subway cars, and smaller automobiles; manufacturers of these products should benefit.

However, the airlines represent the only realistic avenue of investment for anyone wanting to put money into passenger transportation. The railroads are unlikely to reenter the passenger market except through Amtrak, and there is only one publicly owned intercity bus company (Greyhound) and most of its earnings actually derive from nontransportation activities.

If history is any guide, airline earnings will continue to be volatile during the 1980s, depending largely upon traffic and capacity growth. In view of this uncertain outlook, you must be highly selective when investing in the airline industry. First, you want an airline which has a modern, fuel-efficient, and cost-effective fleet of aircraft, as well as a strong balance sheet to finance additional aircraft either from internally generated funds or from debt. (Most airlines sell below book value per share and any equity financing would dilute the ownership of existing shareholders.) Another important competitive advantage for an airline would be to have a large share of traffic flows into or out of major regional centers, which can offer an airline the potential to extend its route network into new geographic market areas, building on its control of the regional center.

Airlines that can meet all of the above criteria have the opportunity to achieve long-term earnings growth. They will be able to gain market shares over competitors because of their ability to finance additional capacity. Airlines that do not meet these criteria will be forced to contract operations and lose market share.

By these standards, the greatest market share gainer should be *Delta Airlines*. The company has the requisite modern, fuel-efficient aircraft fleet and possesses a strong regional identity and a strong base — Atlanta. It has enjoyed good labor relations (its labor force, with the exception of the pilots, is nonunion) and its policy of not laying off employees in slow times has created a high level of loyalty. Delta has a strong balance sheet and a financial position that will allow it to expand with internally generated funds at a time when most other airlines are already debt-heavy and are being squeezed by interest costs. It will face more competition in its traditional markets, but, because of its ability to add aircraft, it should be a market share gainer. Delta has been expanding slowly into new markets with a well-planned strategy. Its current plan is to establish another Atlanta-like hub in the Dallas-Fort Worth area.

BEST LONG-TERM INVESTMENTS: TRANSPORTATION CONGLOMERATES

By 1990 the first of the super freight transportation companies should be emerging. These conglomerates will be able to handle the total transportation needs of shippers, allowing each customer to choose from an extensive range of services and fees. Next-day service, for example, will be one price, one-week service will be cheaper, and quantity discounts will be offered for large-volume regular shipments.

It will also be important for such conglomerates to offer a full range of services in every market and to manage pickup and delivery operations so that many small shipments can be efficiently consolidated into full-capacity loads for longer distances.

In addition, these conglomerates will need sophisticated computerized management information systems and excellent controls over what will become large, complex operations. They must also have access to large amounts of capital to finance the newest equipment, since minute improvements in energy efficiency and productivity can yield big returns.

Guessing what companies of today will be the transportation conglomerates of the 1990s is the real investment challenge, and the one with the biggest payoff for the long term. In that regard, the railroads are most likely to succeed. The lower cost of rail and its importance as a base for any type of large transportation enterprise suggests that the railroads will become an essential part of the transportation conglomerate of tomorrow. Investment in railroad stock looks to us like the best way to catch a ride on the freight transportation of the future.

CHAPTER 12

Health Care

There isn't an American today who isn't aware of the spiraling cost of health care. Any prolonged illness or debilitating disease not covered by insurance or other forms of aid could strain most families' resources and devour capital voraciously.

The crisis in health care costs stems partly from government's decision to enter the health care field through Medicare and Medicaid, as well as from the increasing pervasiveness of third-party insurance provided employees. This gave people the impression that health care was "free" and didn't cost anything. In other words, the relative price of health care declined, and as usually happens, consumption increased dramatically, thereby driving up costs.

Obviously, health care costs can't continue to skyrocket. Public concern over rising costs for hospital services has reached a crescendo. The delivery of quality care in a cost-efficient manner is now clearly the major objective of our health care system.

What's the solution? The main hope lies in the private sector and the health care delivery companies, or what is often called the hospital management industry. This may surprise many people who are mainly familiar with city-owned local hospitals. But, in certain locations around the country, professionally managed, for-profit hospital chains are actually doing a good job of controlling the rise in hospital costs.

In the huge $250 billion-a-year health care industry, there is obviously much room for elimination of waste, increased competition, and introduction of technology and modern business management practices. As competition and professional management are introduced to the industry, we expect two major trends to occur:

1. *Decentralization.* The high cost of hospitalization will encourage the delivery of more and more health-related functions outside of the hospital. In time, the hospital will be used primarily for surgery.
2. *Consolidation.* Unity of scale and greater efficiencies will bring about mergers and increased market share for certain large-scale providers of health care.

We think there are three sectors within the health care industry that stand to benefit from the trend toward decentralization and / or consolidation: the for-profit hospital management industry, the psychiatric hospital management industry, and clinical laboratory chains. Let's take a closer look at each area and find out what companies are best situated to benefit.

HOSPITAL MANAGEMENT INDUSTRY

Hospital expenditures are the largest single portion of health care, accounting for 39.7 percent of health care spending in 1980. And because of the enormous expense of a hospital stay, controlling hospital costs has become the number-one priority in health care, a goal reinforced by the Reagan administration's new policies.

These policies seek, for instance, to restore competition and advocate a free-enterprise approach whenever possible. Also important, in addition to the Administration's opposition to national health insurance, are the cuts in the federal budget affecting funding for Medicaid and other health care-related spending. Clearly, a reduction of the federal government's involvement in the financial side of health care, which accounts for 28.8 percent of all health spending, will improve the environment for the hospital management industry. If the trend in health care is toward shifting the burden of funding to private insurers and consumers, then costs will become a major factor in hospital selection, if a choice exists. That, in turn, will benefit those hospitals that are professionally managed and work hard at controlling costs.

Another important plus is that this shift in government policy has lessened two major investor concerns about the industry — that government interference would reduce profitability and that a highly regulated industry had limited growth possibilities. Now, the need to reduce government spending and to control costs gives a very important raison d'être for the professionally managed hospital chains.

The hospital management industry will garner an increasing share of the hospital care business in the country. (The management companies can expand their market share through acquisition, new construction, and contracts to provide special services to nonaffiliated hospitals. Also, numerous opportunities exist to improve upon the shortcomings of the current hospital system, in which some one third of all hospitals in the country need renovation or total replacement.)

When you consider how small a percentage of total hospital care is accounted for by the hospital management companies, you can appreciate the growth opportunities. As you can see from Table 16, the for-profit hospitals represent only 10 percent of the total in the country. What other industry in America has inefficient, high-cost competition that accounts for 90 percent of the market?

Table 16

U.S. MARKET SHARES OF HOSPITAL INDUSTRY

	Number of hospitals	%	Number of beds	%
Nonprofit	5,740	82	1,240,455	90
For-profit	1,275	18	140,545	10
Total	7,015	100	1,381,000	100

So far, the hospital chains have focused their expansion in the South, Southwest, and West, regions where some 75 percent of their hospitals are located. Thus, only about 35 percent of the states in the nation account for most of the for-profit hospitals.

There's a simple explanation for this. The states chosen by the for-profit hospitals have attractive economic advantages. Generally speaking, both the local population and economy are growing and local regulators are against bureaucratic controls on health care providers.

Despite the concentration of for-profit hospitals in the South, Southwest, and West, there's still tremendous potential for growth there. For-profit hospitals only account for 25 percent of existing hospitals in these regions. Other factors favoring continued growth are: an abundance of small towns where hospital competition is limited; local economic stability; the existence of many small hospitals which require expansion (and eventually more specialized medical procedures); and support from local communities.

What about the regions that don't have many for-profit hospitals? What is the potential for expansion there? On the face of it, the generally less attractive growth opportunities and often more rigid regulatory environments of these states suggest limited potential. But on a closer observation, the prospects are quite encouraging. For example, private take-overs of municipal hospitals are increasing, particularly where taxpayer support is insufficient to maintain the hospital.

This trend is bound to gather force. In view of inflation, government budget cutbacks, and the spreading national taxpayer's revolt, many local community hospitals are finding themselves in desperate financial straits.

Equally important, physicians and community members in many cases favor the for-profit hospitals, especially where greater financial resources are required to expand or improve existing community medical facilities. Also, local pressure for more efficiency and control over costs is growing more and more intense.

All of these factors favor the growth of the for-profit chains.

Major changes in the structure of health care delivery in the United States are inevitable. But most of the possibilities will require capital and new investment dollars, as well as talented people to manage new systems. While government policy will be likely to provide the main impetus to change, skilled management of for-profit hospitals will be necessary to accomplish the nation's health care goals.

WHY THE CHAINS ARE MORE EFFICIENT

Let's see exactly how much more efficient the chains are in comparison to their not-for-profit counterparts. Table 17 compares what

we believe are the financial operating characteristics of the average
for-profit hospital with those of the nonprofit community institution.

The key point here is that the management of salaried employees
accounts for much of the difference. Payroll and worker benefits account for 50 percent of total expenses at the nonprofit community
hospital and only 42 percent at the for-profit one.

Table 17

AVERAGE FINANCIAL OPERATING STRUCTURES FOR HOSPITALS

	% Total	
	For-profit	Nonprofit
Revenues		
Room and board	35	38
Ancillary services	66	64
Other	1	1
Less bad debts	(2)	(3)
Total	100	100
Expenses		
Payroll	42	50
Benefits	18	21
Supplies and equip.	10	6
Special fees	22	23
Other overhead	8	–
Income	100	100

However, it would be unfair to suggest that nonprofit community
hospitals are as inefficient in their control of labor costs as these estimates suggest. One should remember that a sizable number of nonprofit institutions operate in large cities where pressures from
inflation, unions, and worker turnovers are most pronounced. Many
for-profit hospitals, on the other hand, operate in favorable geographical areas, which allow flexibility in worker scheduling, part-
time assignments, and other labor-related matters.

Another reason why the for-profit hospitals have better control of
payroll expenses is their comparatively low employment of doctors,

as you can see from Table 18. The nonprofit hospitals employ an astounding 9.5 times more full-time doctors than do the for-profit hospitals. For-profit hospitals are also more active in specialized therapeutic and diagnostic services, which are large profit centers for hospitals.

Table 18

PROFESSIONAL EMPLOYMENT BY ACCREDITED COMMUNITY HOSPITALS
(1976)

Category	Hospitals	Full-time physicians, dentists, and residents	Average per hospital
Non-government nonprofit ownership	3,339	50,953	15.3
For-profit ownership	775	1,254	1.6

As in all businesses, the key to controlling costs and providing efficient, quality hospital care is management. And this is where the for-profit chains are at a great advantage over the nonprofit hospitals.

In effect, the fundamental difference between the two is professional management, which exists in depth in the chains and only superficially at the nonprofit hospitals.

The chains have not only a variety of executive talent, but also large staffs with expertise in reimbursement analysis and marketing. The nonprofit sector, especially the small-to-medium-sized institution, normally finds it impossible to attract or compensate management to the same extent as the for-profit sector.

Another plus for the chains is their access to large amounts of new capital — which, in most cases, is not available to their nonprofit counterparts. A continued theme throughout this book is the importance of capital in meeting the challenges of the 1980s. Those companies that have it and are able to purchase the latest productivity-enhancing technology will find themselves at a clear advantage over the competition.

HOSPITAL CHAINS ARE WELL POSITIONED FOR THE 1980S

Growth for the hospital chains will come from other areas besides increased market share. There's potential for increased patient occupancy and number of beds at existing facilities; greater emphasis on the more profitable specialized services; new medical services added to existing facilities; management contracts with hospitals outside the system; and consulting services offered to other hospitals, to name a few.

Opportunities also exist for expansion into treatment of nonacute or chronic illnesses at nonhospital locations. Eventually, the progressive hospital management system will have a series of profitable subsegments, such as after-hospital care or treatment, kidney dialysis, psychiatric therapy, nutritional therapy, home health care personnel assistance, minor surgery, and so forth.

These subsegments have good prospects because health care is always less expensive away from the hospital. Thus, these additional services can be offered at reduced prices, thereby opening up the market.

Another dramatic growth opportunity for the industry is international expansion. In fact, some of the chains are in the process of becoming expert in the delivery of health care worldwide. During the next decade they'll expand from their current base in the United States into multinational giants providing a wide variety of health care services.

While the for-profit hospital industry in general has been growing about 15 percent annually in revenues, the major chains have exceeded this rate because of aggressive expansion strategies. With continuing opportunities and high visibility for the future, the industry leaders could experience the fastest growth within the entire health care field through the mid-1980s.

The outlook for the industry is also enhanced by rising demand. Population growth and an increasingly older population with a greater incidence of hospitalization, more comprehensive private health insurance programs, new services created by advances in medical technology, and greater awareness of opportunities in health care through social and educational influences all contribute to this trend.

Another attractive feature of the industry is consistency and visibility of earnings. Since the demand for hospital services remains strong, the level of hospital activity is predictable. Careful analysis of population growth in an area usually permits a fairly accurate assessment of a hospital's revenue stream over a specified period of time. Furthermore, investors don't have to worry about competition between hospital management companies since federal laws prohibit new hospital construction unless inadequacies of a local hospital can be clearly demonstrated.

THE COMPANIES

The positive atmosphere described above augurs well for *American Medical International* (*AMI*), *Hospital Corp. of America,* and *Humana Inc.,* the three largest publicly held hospital chains.

To summarize their key advantages: American Medical International has the most exciting diversification possibilities and the lowest debt-to-equity ratio in an industry characterized by debt-weighted balance sheets. Hospital Corp. of America has the best historical record of growth and probably the greatest depth of management as well. Humana could have the fastest rate of earnings growth of the three because of its financial and operating leverage.

American Medical International is the most diversified of all the chains. A pioneer in international expansion and the offering of specialized services, AMI continues to look for future growth in these areas, as well as further expansion via hospital acquisition. AMI is putting a lot of emphasis on foreign markets, which has already resulted in health service contracts with certain underdeveloped countries. What's more, the company is strong in both technical and consulting services, booming areas since there is such pressure to control costs.

Hospital Corp. of America has been quite aggressive in expanding through acquisition. In 1979, for instance, about one third of the estimated increase in revenue growth of the company's U.S. operations came from acquisitions.

Over the next several years, Hospital Corp. will probably continue to add to its U.S.-owned hospital base at a rate of approximately 5 – 10 percent annually. This may sound like a lot of acquisitions, but it should be easily achievable.

Normal expansion for the company would involve from five to ten new hospital purchases a year, and many more hospitals than that may actually become available. Independent hospitals are being influenced to sell for financial and / or regulatory compliance considerations; they are also becoming aware of their value to potential purchasers both as a local community franchise and in terms of the cost of duplicating the facility. Enough hospitals should become available so that Hospital Corp. can choose those best suited to its strategic requirements. The company is also vigorously exploring international opportunities.

Hospital Corp. has emphasized management depth and employee training. In October 1978 Donald S. MacNaughton, previously chairman and chief executive officer of Prudential Insurance (before retiring), was appointed chairman of the board and chief executive officer of Hospital Corp. Mr. MacNaughton's arrival not only brought to the company his experience of running a giant organization, but raised the credibility of growth opportunities in the entire investor-owned hospital industry.

Humana Inc.'s financial and operating leverage is much greater than that of any of the other major hospital chains. Its debt / equity ratio is 75 / 25, which is much greater than that of the rest of the industry and must be viewed with caution in these unsettled times. And its hospitals' recent occupancy rate of 57 percent is below the levels of the other major chains, and well below the 74 percent national average. (This lower rate of occupancy reflects the "youth" of Humana's beds — approximately one third have been in place less than five years.)

Humana should therefore be able to leverage its existing hospitals by increasing occupancy rates and revenues "per patient day" as the population in a given area rises and / or a hospital gains market share.

Also, Humana should continue to capitalize on the trend toward greater utilization of outpatient services. For example, the company is emphasizing surgery that can be performed without an overnight stay for the patient. This should have widespread appeal because it eliminates the cost of room and board and because both patients and surgeons find it convenient.

PSYCHIATRIC HOSPITAL MANAGEMENT INDUSTRY

The same trends that favor the for-profit hospital management industry are also at work in the psychiatric hospital business. Ability to deliver psychiatric care in a cost-efficient manner and access to capital resources that permit expansion and modernization of treatment centers assure the professionally managed companies of an increasing share of market.

The industry has some clear advantages even over the professionally managed general hospital sector:

• Well-run psychiatric hospitals have a much better return on invested capital. For instance, the cost of constructing and equipping the average psychiatric hospital is $40,000 per bed, as against $100,000 per bed for the general hospital. (Psychiatric hospitals resemble nursing homes. They are usually one-story structures with patient rooms, conference areas, and space for medical personnel. By contrast, general hospitals have expensive customized sections for surgery and ancillary medical services. Equipment needed at a psychiatric center is minimal, whereas a general hospital requires sophisticated hardware and extensive inventories of medical supplies.) What's more, labor costs are lower: the number of hospital employees per patient in a psychiatric hospital runs 1.8 to 1, as against twice that number for the general hospital.

These relatively modest capital needs and labor costs give the psychiatric hospital very favorable operating leverage. As patient occupancy increases, a larger and larger portion of revenues can be brought down to the bottom line. For example, in a recent fiscal year, Community Psychiatric Centers, one of the best companies in the industry, had a 74.5 percent pretax margin with 58 percent occupancy, as against a 9.3 percent pretax margin for Hospital Corp. with a 67.6 percent occupancy rate.

• Psychiatric hospitals have a much better revenue mix than do the general hospitals. The psychiatric hospitals derive only 15 – 20 percent of their revenues from a cost-based reimbursement system, as against 50 percent for the general hospital. Thus, cost controls or attempts to reduce costs will have less of an effect on the psychiatric hospitals. And price increases can be passed along much more easily, which means better profitability.

The psychiatric hospitals should continue to record good growth. For one thing, these hospitals will get an increasing share of mentally disturbed patients, and overall demand for psychiatric help may rise as well, given greater social awareness of problems and the availability of cures.

Also, like the hospital management companies, these enterprises can expand by constructing new hospitals or acquiring existing ones. The restrictions on putting up new hospitals are starting to ease after a long period of stringency. And the free-standing nature of the psychiatric hospital makes it attractive to both patient and doctor alike. (Doctors like a facility entirely devoted to a specialty, and patients feel less institutionalized in a small hospital than in a large general hospital.) What's more, private psychiatric hospitals owned and operated by psychiatrists are scattered all over the United States, and represent potentially attractive acquisition targets.

Community Psychiatric Centers is the largest publicly owned operator of psychiatric hospitals and runs a chain of kidney dialysis centers as well. The company presently operates sixteen hospitals with a total of 1,417 beds, located mainly in California.

In the future, Community Psychiatric should diversify into two related areas with good growth: alcohol and drug abuse rehabilitation. Psychiatric treatment for both requires the same kind of counseling the company already provides, and expansion into these services would thus be natural. Community Psychiatric could also expand through acquisition of other hospitals, the construction of new facilities, and entry into international markets.

CLINICAL LABORATORY CHAINS

The large, highly automated commercial clinical laboratories should also continue to gain market share. The increasing cost of laboratory work and the introduction of new, highly sophisticated testing equipment favors the well-capitalized chain that can afford to modernize.

This $15 billion-a-year industry is experiencing the same type of consolidation as the hospital management and psychiatric hospital industries. Unfortunately, the number of pure plays in the clinical lab field is quite limited. A well-positioned company is *Biomedical Reference Laboratories, Inc.* Its business is growing, thanks to a number of factors. For one thing, the company is getting new accounts, both in existing markets and through geographical expansion. (For instance, it recently began operations in Texas.) Furthermore, the need for medical testing in general should become greater as more and more people adopt preventive health measures.

The company is also growing through acquisition. Its strategy is to buy an operation in its existing market or one very nearby, thereby strengthening its own position and achieving unity of scale by closing the acquired laboratory and transferring the established accounts to a regional testing center. (Occasionally, however, the company will keep a laboratory open, if it can be used as a new regional center.)

GENETIC ENGINEERING INDUSTRY

No discussion of opportunities in health care would be complete without a reference to genetic engineering. In fact, if one takes the long view, the most exciting development in the whole field of health care is the research into how the cell transmits knowledge through generations.

Several landmark achievements in biology during the late 1930s laid the foundation for subsequent investigation of the precise pathways on which information is passed from one generation to the next in all living systems. This work, taking place principally in academic laboratories in Britain and the United States, has led to a series of brilliant discoveries in genetics, perhaps the most famous being the Nobel Prize-winning work of the molecular biologists James D. Watson and Francis Crick at Cambridge University in the early 1950s.

The new findings have now been condensed into a systematic

body of knowledge pertaining to the way genetic information is coded and transmitted. From a commercial standpoint, this knowledge can be used for commercial purposes, for example, to develop methods of changing the genetic information in a cell and thereby redirecting the cell to produce totally different end products.

The genetic engineering, or gene-splicing, industry, as it is variously called, is in the very early stages of harnessing and commercializing this exceptionally powerful technology. We estimate that, from a virtually standing start in 1975, more than $500 million has been directly invested in the genetic engineering field.

The development of this industry will follow a slow but strongly upward course. Many companies, both very large and very small, are now conducting substantial programs in genetic research, with more entering the field almost every month. The dollar revenues of the genetic engineering business will initially be small, but will grow at exponential rates once several critical cost and process bottlenecks are overcome, probably in the mid-1980s.

We can see a market for genetically derived products of $1 – 2 billion by 1990, rising to perhaps ten times that level by the year 2000. The critical hurdle will not be passed, however, until the mid-1980s. Consequently, we believe that only those companies with strong financial support and a broad base of projects will survive the inevitable consolidation.

The normal financial disciplines imposed by free market mechanisms do not now apply to the genetic engineering field. Large amounts of capital — what seems today to be an unlimited quantity — have been made available to the genetics industry. In our opinion, however, this is a short-lived phenomenon that will gradually fade as investors recognize both the length of time required to produce a big payoff and the speculative, poorly organized character of many firms now in this industry.

Technological change will continue to occur at a rapid pace in a science that is still in its infancy. This will make forward planning difficult, create rapid shifts in specific companies' technical positions, and complicate the decision-making process in committing the very large amounts of money necessary to implement certain potential uses of genetic technology.

One strategy for participating in genetic engineering is to focus on those strongly capitalized drug companies with the greatest research-and-development efforts and resources. The company that seems best to meet these requirements is *Merck & Co.,* one of the major old-line drug concerns. Merck has long been regarded as one of the preeminent firms in the U.S. pharmaceutical industry, and rightly so, since it is the largest in the industry, spends more on research and development than other companies, and has one of the best-organized and largest sales organizations. Despite these strengths, Merck is often perceived as a company with a maturing product line and generally poor growth prospects.

As the facts unfold, however, we believe that a different picture will emerge. Merck is probably entering a period quite similar to 1963 – 67, when earnings rose at a 22 percent compound rate, powered by a wave of new products from Merck's research laboratories. Through the mid-1980s, Merck will probably be the leader in new product development.

For those who are more speculatively inclined and interested in an investment in genetic engineering, *Genentech* is worth taking a look at. So far, it is the premier company in genetics engineering and has the strongest record of solid technological achievement. Already beyond the start-up stage, it has a group of actual products moving toward the marketplace.

We believe that Genentech's business plan has been thought through carefully. As a result, the company has established goals and standards against which the success of each specific project can be measured; many of these projects have now reached the point where the basic science has been worked out and the commercialization stage lies immediately ahead.

CHAPTER 13

Specialty Retailing

In the first three decades after World War II, the retailing industry in the United States grew rapidly as incentives to spend and consume became widespread. But the 1980s are likely to be different. The consumer is not in good financial shape and is unlikely to be the leading edge of economic growth.

In the late 1970s the consumer sector of the economy accelerated spending, financing it with debt and reduced savings. This left consumers overextended because liquidity was viewed as less important than hedging against inflation. The implication is that we are in for a long period of consumer underspending, as liquidity is rebuilt and debt reduced. What's more, a shift in national priorities will reinforce this trend, as Americans see the need for investment and savings, particularly to produce domestic energy and develop technology that will raise productivity. As shown in Table 19, personal consumption as a percent of disposable income has been rising steadily since the mid-1970s.

This burst of consumer spending was financed by borrowing more and saving less. The national savings rate, as shown in Table 20, gives a good idea of what has happened in recent years. On average, the savings rate has remained at historically low levels since the mid-1970s.

The trend toward increased borrowing is just as bleak. In the late 1970s consumer debt as a percent of disposable income rose steadily, as Table 21 illustrates.

Table 19

CONSUMER DISPOSABLE INCOME

| Year | Disposable income ($ billions, 1981) | Total Personal Consumption | |
		Expenditures ($ billions, 1981)	% disposable income
1968	588.2	535.9	91.1
1969	630.4	579.7	92.0
1970	686.0	618.8	90.2
1971	742.8	668.2	90.0
1972	801.3	733.0	91.5
1973	901.6	809.9	89.8
1974	984.6	889.6	90.4
1975	1,086.7	979.1	90.1
1976	1,184.5	1,089.9	92.0
1977	1,305.1	1,210.0	92.7
1978	1,458.4	1,350.8	92.6
1979	1,698.0	1,579.1	93.0
1980	1,810.3	1,683.6	93.0
1981	2,010.4	1,859.6	92.5

Table 20

SAVINGS RATE

Year	%
1972	6.2
1973	7.8
1974	7.3
1975	7.7
1976	5.8
1977	5.0
1978	5.0
1979	5.0
1980	5.3
1981	5.2

Table 21

CREDIT EXTENSIONS AS A PERCENT OF DISPOSABLE INCOME

Year	%
1970	16.75
1971	18.55
1972	19.05
1973	19.19
1974	17.52
1975	16.58
1976	17.73
1977	19.47
1978	20.47
1979	20.00
1980	16.5
1981	17.0

Table 22

REAL DISPOSABLE PERSONAL INCOME

Year	Real disposable income ($ billions)	% year-to-year change
1965	612.6	–
1966	643.6	5.1
1967	669.8	4.1
1968	695.1	3.8
1969	712.7	2.5
1970	741.4	4.0
1971	769.3	3.8
1972	801.3	4.2
1973	854.5	6.6
1974	842.0	−1.5
1975	859.7	2.1
1976	891.9	3.7
1977	929.4	4.2
1978	972.6	4.6
1979	994.1	2.2
1980	996.2	0.2
1981	1,031.1	3.5

Essentially, consumers have tried to maintain their standard of living by borrowing and by digging into savings. But in the economic environment we face, this is a losing battle; during 1979–81, average wages significantly lagged behind inflation. Disposable personal income, after adjusting for inflation, rose in each of the last fifteen years, with the exception of the recession year of 1974. As Table 22 shows, 1979–81 were difficult years.

However, consumer spending patterns are not uniform and the demographic profile of a merchant's location is a key ingredient to profit potential. Indeed, we believe that site selection is as important as any function performed by retailers. To this end, we have completed an analysis of the major retail markets in the United States in order to determine which regions and states will probably experience the strongest gains in retail sales during the 1980s.

Our conclusion, which is summarized in the accompanying tables, suggests that most of the South, and particularly Texas, remains very attractive. The Mountain region can also be expected to have excellent consumer spending patterns, having enjoyed steadily improving demographics. On the negative side, the Middle Atlantic and New England (excluding two or three surprising state exceptions) are still the least favorable areas for future spending.

Table 23

REGIONAL MARKET RANKING FOR RETAILING

Extremely favorable	*Moderately favorable*	*Generally unfavorable*
West South Central	East South Central	East North Central
Mountain	Pacific	New England
South Atlantic	West North Central	Middle Atlantic

State-by-state analysis yields good insights also, as is clear from Table 24. It is not a surprise that Florida and Texas appear among the five most favorable states, but it is a surprise that Virginia, Utah, and New Hampshire do. New York, Ohio, the District of Columbia, Pennsylvania, and Rhode Island are the least favorable areas. While the once "hot" areas such as Arizona, California, and Nevada remain moderately favorable, they have slipped from their top rankings. On the other hand, some northeastern states (e.g., New Jersey and Vermont) have improved in recent years and an interesting collection of border areas like Kentucky and Oklahoma are included in the extremely favorable ranking.

Table 24

STATE MARKET RANKINGS FOR RETAILERS

Extremely favorable	Moderately favorable	Generally unfavorable
Florida	New Mexico	North Dakota
Utah	North Carolina	Delaware
Texas	Maryland	South Dakota
Virginia	Mississippi	Iowa
New Hampshire	Nevada	Minnesota
South Carolina	California	Nebraska
Oregon	Louisiana	Massachusetts
Tennessee	Arizona	Michigan
Alaska	Alabama	Montana
Oklahoma	Washington	Illinois
Colorado	Vermont	Connecticut
Hawaii	New Jersey	Indiana
Kentucky	Missouri	Rhode Island
Idaho	Wisconsin	Pennsylvania
Georgia	Maine	Ohio
Wyoming	Kansas	New York
Arkansas	West Virginia	

Despite the problems discussed above with overall consumer spending, we believe there will be certain long-term changes taking place and pockets of growth in retailing that will offer good investment opportunities:

• Incomes will grow fastest at the upper end of the income spectrum (household income above $50,000 annually).

• The population will get both older and younger. By 1991, one fourth of the nation will be considered senior citizens. At the same time, the number of children six years old or under will grow at a pace one third faster than the total population.

- Geographic shifts will continue. The Mountain, Southwest, and Gulf Coast areas appear to be the most likely areas to show rapid consumer spending growth from population shifts. The Atlantic Coast and West Coast will remain popular, if somewhat crowded. Continued slower growth in the industrial Midwest and Middle Atlantic appear likely.

- Consumer values will be fragmented and increasingly influenced by special interest groups. Customers will shop at more stores, more discriminately.

- Leisure time will become increasingly important. The consumer will often spend on these activities as if they were necessities, while sometimes deferring spending on apparel and other products previously considered necessities.

- Merchandise will have greater technological flavor.

- Product specialization will continue. Specialty retailing will increasingly emphasize narrower product mixes. At the same time, many more nonproduct consumer services will be offered in retail outlets.

The important investment implications of these major trends are that two types of retailing companies will be attractive: those that sell a very essential product and those that sell a very exciting one. Within these two broad categories, we believe there are a number of subsegments with attractive growth opportunities:

Very essential

Economic advantage retailers
Food retailers
Health care retailers

Very exciting

Consumer electronics retailers
Retailers serving growing population segments
Companies serving consumers that have little sensitivity to the
    economy

Economic advantage retailers. Increasing portions of consumer income will be drained by energy, housing, and service expenses. The consumer will, therefore, continue to seek ways to conserve income while maintaining the use of major assets like the house and car. Those companies that can give the consumer an economic break relative to inflation and help him or her to avoid asset deterioration or future expense will be increasingly popular. As a result, the whole gamut of do-it-yourself merchandise will provide a unique opportunity for the consumer to build a hedge against tough times.

The broadest category of do-it-yourself merchandise is found in the home center business. Home centers provide a wide range of products designed to help customers maintain or improve their largest asset, the house. In our opinion, these merchants are barely tapping many potential areas (security and energy, for instance) and can rapidly expand their customer impact. Note the following:

• Home center product demand is expanding relatively quickly and large numbers of new products are introduced every year.

• The cost of a do-it-yourself project is significantly lower than the cost of one using skilled labor, and the gap is widening.

• Home center chains have barely tapped the market. The top ten companies still represent less than 6 percent of total industry sales. Chains should continue to take market share from local dealers, hardware merchants, and lumber yards.

• In some ways, the home center has become a provider of leisure time activity. For certain people, tinkering with the house can replace other more expensive activities.

• The home center industry is one of the few retail sectors experiencing annual store expansion.

• Many home center products are not easily price-compared. While this is obviously less true for professional builders than infrequent customers, it does allow a good deal of flexibility in passing on costs.

Food. Retailers in this field have not enjoyed much investor sponsorship in past years, primarily because of volatile competitive patterns and commodity costs. However, these companies could now develop earnings gains that are more stable, and perhaps consistently better, than the leading general merchants because of the following reasons:

- Demand for food is relatively stable. Certain families may alter consumption patterns, but the underlying market does not change dramatically.
- Food retailers have historically done well in tough economic times.

We believe that rapidly growing, well-managed food retailers can take advantage of these trends. The best example is *Dillon Companies*, one of the nation's leading regional food chains. Dillon operates more than 215 supermarkets, over 330 convenience stores, and 20 junior department stores in California, the Mountain and West South Central regions, and the farmbelt. The company's record is impressive. For the ten years ending in June 1981, Dillon's annual sales and earnings rose by 22 percent and 19 percent, respectively.

Dillon is the first- or second-ranked supermarket in most of its operating areas and is a particularly tough competitor in Colorado and Kansas. Its sales volume is derived almost exclusively from parts of the country projected to have above national-average income growth.

Health Care. Physical fitness and health maintenance are more than passing fads — they and related leisure-time activities embody current consumer preferences. People are spending and will continue to spend larger portions of their income dollars on these activities. Companies selling health care products often generate high margins, usually appeal to above-average income and education groups, and offer constant opportunities for an expanding customer base.

Improved health care and life styles are increasing longevity, and this, coupled with the aging of the population, is rapidly increasing the number of senior citizens in the United States. By 1990 seniors may represent one quarter of the total population. While many of these people are on fixed incomes, their sheer numbers provide an opportunity for retail sales.

While few companies specifically service this senior population, drug chains benefit from both young children and seniors — the heaviest prescription drug users. We anticipate prescription drug use to increase at a more rapid pace through the mid-1980s than they have since 1975. This is particularly important to drug chains since prescription drugs usually constitute one of the most profitable product areas. Over-the-counter health aids will also benefit from these population groups.

Consumer Electronics. The most obvious example of strong retail demand occurs in areas of consumer technology and electronics. There is general agreement that merchants have barely tapped the future technology and have yet to merchandise most current electronic fields fully. Consumer electronics retailers, for example, enjoy the highest growth in the industry and can reasonably expect the highest unit demand growth as well. This allows them a great deal of high-margin merchandising flexibility in items that are not easily price-compared. The leading companies will undoubtedly use price as an offensive weapon — as they have with calculators and games — in order to keep operations expensive for competitors.

Retailers Serving Growing Population Segments. Earlier we noted that overall population and household growth will be minimal through the 1980s. This is not to suggest, however, that all population segments or areas will stagnate. Indeed, as we have implied, some clear growth pockets exist that will significantly outpace overall industry changes.

For example, recent increases in monthly live births indicate a mini baby boom. The number of children under the age of six should rise at a pace one-third faster than the overall population during the next five to ten years. Changing attitudes, a return to family orientation, and the twenty-five-to-thirty-five-year baby boom bulge are all contributing to a growing young population.

We think that the toy business is an obvious way to take advantage of new child births. The toy supermarket not only services an important population segment, but does so at economically attractive prices.

Toys R Us is the largest and most successful toy retailer in the country. The company operates 101 stores and is rapidly expanding. A typical store, averaging 45,000 square feet in floor space, features a wide selection of children's toys and furniture, sporting equipment, and related items.

The company's toy supermarkets have as yet barely begun to realize their potential; despite having gained market share from competitors, these stores are still in less than 15 percent of the nation's major markets. These stores are increasingly important providers of popular electronic gadgetry (as we have seen, an expanding area), and have plenty of room to grow in since they only account for a small portion of total toy sales at present.

Companies Serving Consumers That Have Little Sensitivity to the Economy. Certain consumers are far less sensitive to price increases than others. Households with earnings of $50,000 are the most rapidly growing income segment. These consumers often benefit both from dual paychecks and from good compensation increases. They are not as troubled, therefore, by product price increases and have much greater discretionary spending power. Therefore, we think retailers serving high-income consumers will do well.

Nordstrom, Inc., is one of the most successful fashion specialty store merchants in the country. It operates thirty-two department stores, primarily in the Northwest, which stress medium- to high-quality fashion merchandise. These stores are very attractive and exciting to visit.

The company has strong market positions and is a leader in all of its older markets. So far, Nordstrom has been successful whenever it enters a new market. It plans to continue aggressive expansion, already having moved into Los Angeles and Salt Lake City. By 1985 it will be in at least four or five new markets.

CHAPTER 14

The Bottom Line

To sum up, there are certain changes going on in the economy that may have a profound effect on one's investments and financial situation, even one's career. We believe that these changes are of a long-term nature, and that they are occurring subtly and slowly. One cannot comprehend or deal with these developments with a superficial knowledge. An in-depth understanding is essential. To wit:

1. After this recession ends, we may enter a long period of economic growth, low inflation, rising stock prices, and opportunities for business persons and entrepreneurs. The outlook for energy price stability is the best it's been in a decade. Technology is invading our economy and offers the prospects of some improvement in productivity. Government economic policy is apparently making a major switch toward favoring free enterprise. Industries representing as much as 50 percent of GNP are in various stages of deregulation. For the first time in many years, there appears to be a limit on increases in government spending. And the Reagan administration has in its ranks several expert "Fed watchers," which suggest monetary policy will remain moderate.

2. Runaway inflation appears most unlikely. The popularity of hyperinflation advice in 1979 – 80 and early 1981 suggests to "contrary" thinkers that disinflation is probable.

3. Stocks may be a good investment once the transition to disinflation has occurred, with potential returns that could be considered high by historical standards. Not only is the stock market already at historically low valuations, but an economic recovery, when it comes in late 1983 or 1984, could bring higher p / e multiples for the stock market as a whole.

4. Changes in relative prices are creating unit growth opportunities for ten new industries: personal automation hardware, video entertainment, office automation, information vending, factory electronics, energy producers, energy services, the deregulation of transportation, and specialty retailing. Historically, the major determinant of business success has been a relative price advantage — which usually generates huge increases in volume. We have tried to emphasize those parts of the economy that appear to have some form of relative price advantage. We believe that an understanding of the relative price changes taking place in the economy is essential for everyone. One's job, business, and the performance of one's investments will be heavily influenced by how well one incorporates such changes into one's personal business and investment life.

5. Certain companies appear to be well positioned to take advantage of these changes in relative price, either because of good fortune, foresight, good management, or all three. We have attempted to identify those companies that have a strategic business plan aimed at capitalizing on the growth opportunities in these ten new industries. Undoubtedly, we have missed many future success stories, and some of our candidates may prove disappointing because of a failure to realize their full potential or a competitive shift that they were slow to respond to. Also, the transition to disinflation may prove difficult for many of these companies, especially those with fast growth rates and leveraged balance sheets. But the group as a whole should provide a blueprint for those who wish to monitor the developments in some or all of these new industries.

Index